Your
Cat
Interpreter

Your Cat Interpreter

How to Understand What Your Cat Is Telling You

David Alderton

Reader's Digest

The Reader's Digest Association, Inc.
Pleasantville, New York / Montreal

A READER'S DIGEST BOOK

This edition published by The Reader's Digest Association, Inc., by arrangement with Cico Books, an imprint of Ryland, Peters and Small
20—21 Jockey's Fields, London WC1R 4BW

FOR CICO BOOKS
Design Jerry Goldie
Editor Marie Clayton
Illustrators Cathy Brear, Trina Dalziel
Photo Credits see page 192

FOR READER'S DIGEST
U.S. Project Editor Kimberly Casey
Canadian Project Editor Pamela Johnson
Project Designer Jennifer Tokarski
Associate Art Director George McKeon
Executive Editor, Trade Publishing Dolores York
Associate Publisher Rosanne McManus
President and Publisher, Trade Publishing
   Harold Clarke

Library of Congress Cataloging-in-Publication Data

Alderton, David, 1956–
   Your cat interpreter : how to understand what your cat is telling you / David Alderton.
      p. cm.
   Includes bibliographical references and index.
   ISBN-13: 978-0-7621-0818-3
   ISBN-10: 0-7621-0818-5
   1. Cats--Behavior. 2. Cats. 3. Human-animal communication. I. Title.
   SF446.5.A35 2006
   636.8--dc22   2006049528

Address any comments about *Your Cat Interpreter* to:
   The Reader's Digest Association, Inc.
   Adult Trade Publishing
   Reader's Digest Road
   Pleasantville, NY 10570-7000

For more Reader's Digest products and information, visit our website:
   www.rd.com (in the United States)
   www.readersdigest.ca (in Canada)

NOTES TO OUR READERS
The advice given here should not be used as a substitute for that of a qualified veterinarian. No cats or kittens were harmed in the making of this book.

In this book, unless the information given is specifically for male cats, cats are referred to as "she." The information is equally applicable to male and female cats, unless otherwise specified.

Printed in Singapore

1 3 5 7 9 10 8 6 4 2

Contents

Introduction

Fascination with Felines

Our relationship with cats has lasted for at least 5,000 years—and possibly much longer. At the outset, in ancient Egypt, it was based on mutual benefit. The growth of agriculture meant that large quantities of grain and other food was stored in one place, and this soon attracted rodents. The hunting abilities of the wildcat helped to control the threat of rodents and so, in turn, the presence of the cats was tolerated. Gradually, the wildcat's natural caution of people was overcome, and domestication took root as cats started to move into homes in search of shelter.

The bond in those early days was probably every bit as strong as it is today—cat owners would even shave off their eyebrows as a sign of respect and mourning when a cherished pet died. A cult worshiping cats in all their guises became established in ancient Egypt and lasted for some 2,000 years.

The subsequent relationship between cats and people was not always so straightforward, since the nocturnal nature of the cat led to links with the occult in the fifteenth century. However, by the 1700s the cat's rehabilitation was largely complete. Cats have since provided inspiration for both artists and writers, fascinated by the form and character of these remarkable creatures.

On a basic level, domestic cats retain many of the attributes that make their wild relatives such effective hunters. They possess a formidable array of senses, combined with natural athletic prowess and remarkable coordination. Despite this, they are quite content to share our homes—and the fact that we know they could survive quite well on their own without us, but actively choose to remain, makes the relationship more meaningful.

The Image Of The Cat
The resourceful, adaptable, and intelligent nature of cats was appreciated at an early stage in history. It is perhaps best summarized in the

In the past, domestic cats regularly had to roam and hunt for their own food outdoors. Prepared cat foods are a relatively recent development, dating back less than a century.

popular European fairy tale *Puss in Boots*—also sometimes known as *The Master Cat*. This formed one of eight popular children's tales (also including *Cinderella* and *Little Red Riding Hood*) that together were published in France in a book entitled *Stories or Tales from Times Past, with Morals*. Even then—in 1697—these stories were well-known in Europe, but Charles Perrault's retelling of them in this form struck a sympathetic chord with readers. It is rather ironic, perhaps, that Perrault—who lived from 1628 until 1703—is best-known for these stories today, although he was a leading academic of the period, and published this volume originally under the name of his son, Pierre.

The Story Of Puss In Boots

A miller had three sons and when he died, his eldest son inherited the mill, while his second son was left the donkey. The miller's cat was given to the youngest son, who felt rather let down by this considering the value of what his brothers had received. Nevertheless, the cat was able to talk, and reassured the young man. He asked for a hat, cloak, and boots, as well as a bag, and before setting off to hunt he promised to help his new master become rich.

The cat soon caught a fat rabbit and—unbeknown to his owner—headed off to the nearby King's castle

The colorpoint pattern was established in Asia centuries ago.

In the seventeenth century, the tale of *Puss in Boots* was already well known in Europe.

where he left the rabbit as a gift. Each day he returned with a similar offering, which he gave to the King saying they were from his master, the Marquis of Carabas. Before long, the Marquis's reputation as a man of generosity had spread, but no one knew who he was.

One day, the Queen summoned his messenger and asked if the Marquis was young and handsome, to which the cat replied that he was, adding that he was also a very wealthy man. The cat then invited the King and Queen to visit the Marquis at his castle. When he told the miller's son what had been arranged the poor young man was horrified, but the cunning cat knew what he doing. He arranged for his master to strip off

Cats can form a strong bond with their owners, particularly if they are obtained as kittens.

and swim in the river, just as the royal coach was approaching. It seemed that this would be a disaster because the miller's son was unable to swim, but as the royal coach came near the cat called out that the Marquis was drowning. The King's men rushed to rescue him, and fine new clothes were brought for him to wear. It was love at first sight for the Princess, who was traveling with her parents. She wanted to marry the eligible young Marquis immediately, but first the courtiers determined to find out his true wealth.

The cat then rushed off through the surrounding fields, telling the workers that—on pain of death—they were to say that the Marquis of

Carabas owned all the land. Soon the cat reached a nearby castle, the home of an ogre. The ogre could change form and immediately became a fearsome lion to scare his visitor. The cat responded by saying he had heard the ogre was unable to make himself smaller, suggesting that he should change himself into a rat or mouse to prove this was untrue. When the ogre foolishly did so, the cat pounced and ate the rodent, just before the royal procession reached the castle. The cat welcomed the royal party to the Marquis's castle, and the Marquis and the Princess were married and lived happily ever after.

Truth And Legend

Another well-known tale involving the cat's hunting ability is the story of Dick Whittington—although in this case, the legend is built on a true story. Richard Whittington was the second son of Sir William Whittington, who owned a large estate in the English county of Gloucestershire. When his father died in 1358, the young man traveled to London seeking work. He became an apprentice to a mercer, learning about the trade in precious materials, such as silk, which were imported for wealthy patrons and sold largely in royal circles.

Richard Whittington built up a valuable network of contacts, and once he became a mercer himself he soon became very wealthy—he even lent money to the Crown. He became a City Alderman in 1393 and was subsequently chosen as Lord Mayor of London by Richard II in 1399. He was re-elected to this post on three further occasions, and held it until his death in 1423. Whittington left his fortune to be used to help improve London, and to benefit the poorer people of the city in particular. An almshouse was built for them, and the water supply was improved.

As the years passed, stories began to grow about how Whittington had obtained his fortune—and the story of Dick Whittington and his cat developed. A typical version sees the young man leaving Gloucestershire as a poor boy, and walking to London. Here he finds employment in the home of a wealthy merchant and falls in love with the merchant's beautiful daughter, who was called Alice.

Dick shares his attic lodgings with his cat, who is an excellent mouser. When the merchant asks all his servants if they want to invest in a trading expedition to far-off lands, the only thing that Dick could contribute to the voyage was his cat. After sending his cat away, Dick decides to travel back to Gloucester—but as he pauses on his way out of London, he thinks he hears the city's church bells telling him to turn round and go back. Three times the bells tell him that he will be Lord Mayor of London.

On his return to his former lodgings, he learns that the voyage has been a great success. A great King overseas was so impressed by the rodent-catching skills of his cat that he has paid a very large sum of money to buy the animal—which means that Dick himself is now a very rich man. He marries Alice and becomes Lord Mayor, just as the bells had predicted.

This story became increasingly embellished over time, and has since been performed on stage—usually as a pantomime—with fact and fantasy blended to commemorate one of London's most famous benefactors. Even today, some 600 years later, Whittington's legacy is still evident in the capital through the charity known as the Whittington Trust—even if he never owned a cat!

Sʳ RICHᴰ WITTINGTON,
from an Original Painting at
MERCERS HALL.

A traditional representation of Dick Whittington and his cat—this tale is based on a combination of fact and fantasy.

A non-pedigree kitty is a rewarding and self-reliant friend.

The athletic nature of cats is a subject that has long appealed to artists—not only in the West but also across the East.

from portrayals of cats in art during this period. As early as the 1500s, the famous Italian artist Leonardo da Vinci drew amazing behavioral studies of cats, showing them grooming themselves and playing naturally— rather than using the image of a cat as a symbol. Gradually, across Europe, artists began to incorporate cats into scenes of domestic life, confirming the cat's public rehabilitation.

The era of the specialty cat painter dawned in 1800s. Typical of this genre is the work of Swiss feline artists Gottfried Mind and Henriette Ronner. Ronner's work was especially realistic, because she placed great emphasis on the anatomical charac-teristics of her subject, developing a photo-realistic approach.

Cats soon became popular subjects on calendars and greeting cards, and cute cats appeared on chocolate box lids. This gave rise to an increasingly anthropomorphic view of cats in art as the century drew to a close, which is best seen in the rise of the Catland movement.

As the postal service developed, picture post cards became the fashionable way to communicate and Catland cards provided a novel and amusing way for people to keep in touch. Catland was a world populated entirely by cats, with human characteristics and dress sense—this style of greeting card, in which cats are shown as people, can still be found today. The first artist to

Changing Times

Although *Puss in Boots* and *Dick Whittington* are quite separate stories, the common themes in each give a clear insight into how cats were popularly perceived in medieval Europe. Whereas the Church often inspired their persecution during this time, clearly not everyone was convinced that cats were agents of evil. Instead they were seen in a similar way to how we perceive them today—as both valued companions and resourceful hunters.

As the Renaissance dawned, followed by an age of Enlightenment, the active persecution of cats by the authorities began to cease in Europe. Cats were once again seen only as members of the animal kingdom with adept senses, rather than being regarded as the possessors of super-natural powers. This becomes clear

draw in this style for card publishers Raphael Tuck and Sons was Helen Maguire. Initially, her cats were portrayed wearing bows, but gradually they started to wear clothes and parody human activities.

The artist who became most closely associated with the Catland theme was Louis Wain, who began drawing cats while his wife was bedridden with cancer. His illustrations were based on his own black-and-white non-pedigree cat, Peter, and later appeared in books of children's stories.

Wain became the second president of the United Kingdom's National Cat Club during the 1890s. He began working for Raphael Tuck and Sons in 1902, developing the Catland theme. Its popularity lasted until the 1920s; these cards are in great demand today among collectors. Unfortunately, Louis Wain obtained little benefit from the massive industry that he had helped to establish, suffering increasingly desperate financial circumstances.

While the end of the Catland era marked a change in taste, it was not an indication that cats were falling out of favor as pets. By the latter half of the twentieth century, cats had usurped the dog's traditional role of most popular companion. Today, the cat's popularity with pet-seekers is higher than ever, as increasing numbers of would-be owners are attracted by the appeal of purebred felines. And, of course, our need to communicate and bond with with our cats will always be part of our nature.

Looking at this cute kitten it is very easy to see how the Catland cards, based on an anthropomorphic view of cats, became so popular at the end of the nineteenth century.

How To Bond With
Your Cat

A cat can fit so seamlessly into your life

that it is all too easy to take her for

granted. Your intelligent feline friend

possesses a great capacity to tune

into your emotions, so learning new ways

to respond to her day-to-day needs can

only deepen your mutual bond.

A Caring Bond: The Basics

How we treat a cat from the earliest moments of her life will profoundly influence both her character and inclinations. Kittens, just like babies, are intensely affected by their early environment.

Their eyes open sometime between two and 11 days after birth. At around five weeks they enter a socialization period, which will last up to 12 weeks. The relationships that kittens form during this time are crucial because they determine the nature of their future relationships with both people and felines. Kittens who are adored, picked up, and stroked by people grow up to be happy and affectionate pets. Even if they fall on hard times and are forced into isolation, they retain the capacity and desire for an emotional bond. So even if your cat comes to you at a later stage in life, it is still possible for you to form a close bond with her. When given a good home, with lots of patient and loving care, your cat will blossom.

Bonding With Your New Cat

When you first bring your kitten home she is certain to feel nervous and need reassurance in her new environment, even if she previously received the most tender attention. She has boundaries, and it is important to respect them. Be guided not by how you want to react to your new pet, but by how she reacts to you and the world around her. If you force her into situations that frighten or unnerve her, she will lash out with claws and teeth or run away. Bad experiences can linger in her subtle

Feeling very relaxed and at home in her surroundings, this cat—lying on her back and trying to catch your eye—is also clearly in a playful mood.

feline mind and negatively shape her future behavior and personality.

If you have young children, it is particularly important to supervise them when they have contact with your cat or kitten. Children can badly upset a new kitten, or even an older cat from a rescue center. They may want to pick her up and squeeze her body in an excess of affection or pull her ears in fun, but it is a rare feline who relishes these loving advances. Your cat will feel claustrophobic and frightened, long for escape, and struggle fiercely. She may scratch or bite and she may suffer a heavy, awkward drop to the floor.

If she's old, fat, fragile, or arthritic, she may even be injured. If your kitten or cat associates the attentions of children with being afraid, she will soon avoid them. And if the children think the new family member is going to hurt them if they try to play with her, they will soon begin to dislike her.

Making Her Feel Secure

So how do you behave around this fascinating newcomer? One of the first things your cat needs to learn is that being picked up is not going to be a scary experience. She needs to be approached gently but confidently. Speak softly as you scoop her up, putting one hand around her chest and under her front legs. Use the other hand to steady her as you lift her toward you. Your cat needs to feel secure in your arms, and this means

Cats are instinctively nervous by nature, so you will need to be very patient when you are introducing your pet to unfamiliar sensations, such as being groomed.

her whole body must be supported. If her hindquarters are left dangling in space, she will panic and dig her claws into your arms or another part of your body in an attempt to cling on, just as she would when climbing a tree.

Holding your cat correctly is vital, because there will be times when she will need to be held and carried for practical reasons—such as for trips to the vet, for example. When you have your cat in your arms, hold her firmly but gently. The moment she wants to be free, put her down again; if she anticipates being held against her will, she will do everything possible to avoid being picked up.

Finally, never try to pick up your feline pal before her mealtimes. A hungry cat has only one thing on her mind, and it's not being stroked. It's much better to wait and pick her up and make a fuss over her after dinner, when she is full, happy, sleepy, and languorous.

What Food Means To Your Feline

Feeding your cat is such an every day, routine experience—yet when it is approached correctly, it can rapidly help to advance the wondrous and unique relationship that you and your cat are forging.

Cats, like us, love food. If you leave out large, tempting bowls of cat chow and simply allow her to munch her way through them—just like a chocoholic left with a box of Belgian truffles—she will soon eat them all.

First your cat's waistline will expand a bit, then she will become a little lazy. Soon her waist will expand some more, until suddenly and almost unexpectedly you have an obese, unhealthy cat on your hands.

Try to adjust the amount of food you give your cat to her appetite. She should feel hungry when dinnertime arrives, and eat her food rapidly and enthusiastically. If she doesn't finish it within 10 to 15 minutes, you're probably overfeeding her and need to take the remains away.

All prepared cat food includes feeding guidelines that will initially help you get the amounts more or less right. But remember that cats are individuals. An active, stalking, hunting, outdoor cat needs more calories than one that prefers to curl up next to that warm radiator.

Cats need somewhere quiet to eat. If you need to change her food, start by mixing the two brands together for a few days to minimize the possibility of any loss of appetite or digestive upset.

Establishing A Routine

If you put your cat's food out at the same times every day, her internal body clock will let her know that food should be arriving soon. She will begin to seek you out—behavior that will strengthen the magical bond between you. Typically, she will attract your attention by twining herself around your legs. Some call this cupboard love, for obvious reasons, but it is more significant than this. She is marking your legs with scent from glands on her face, thereby including you in her social group. Of course, if you ignore her when she knows that chow is due, she will meow loudly, incessantly, and demandingly until you fill up that cavernously empty bowl.

You can use mealtimes to begin training your kitten to come when called. If you repeat her name as you give her food, she'll soon recognize your voice, feel a positive association with it, and learn her name. Then establish a routine, such as putting her out in the backyard for a set period of time and then calling her, and she will quickly respond to your voice. Always call your cat with an enthusiastic mellow tone, even if she doesn't respond at once. If you shout or sound angry, she will think that you are going to reprimand her. Who wants to come home only to be scolded? In a few short weeks your

cat will begin to accept this routine as part of her life, so if you are out at the appointed hour, you will return home to find a disgruntled cat sitting on your doorstep.

Giving Rewards

Everyone knows dogs will perform tricks for a treat—sit up and beg, or roll over—but will your cat? Cats are

The Scratching Post
Why Cats Love Their Food

Keep an eye on your cat's appetite, because this can give you clues about her state of health or lifestyle. If she is not eating as much as usual, it could be an early sign of illness—or your pet may have found a tastier source of food nearby! The weather may also affect your cat's appetite, since felines generally eat less when a storm is imminent. A change in the cat's environment or, in the case of an intact tom, the desire to mate can also cause a temporary decline of interest in food.

It makes sense to take advantage of life stage kitten diets, which have been formulated to meet the needs of growing cats.

clever creatures and are far more responsive to training than most of us imagine. Like dogs, cats will come to the table and beg for food. Initially they sit patiently, hoping you will offer them a succulent tidbit, but if this strategy fails, they often stand up on their hind legs and put their front paws on your leg. You're bound to notice them now.

Sitting up and begging—a position halfway between these two postures—occurs when your cat is still resting her weight on her hindquarters but her front paws are raised. If you reward your pet just at this moment, before her front paws come to rest on your leg, she'll promptly revert to her original sitting position to devour the juicy morsel. If you make this into a routine, your canny feline will soon realize that "begging" brings a desirable reward. Agile, compact cats—such as Siamese—find this trick easy.

The look of intense concentration on the face of this young cat as she catches her toy reveals the importance of mastering hunting skills, which would be crucial for her survival in the wild.

But for some cats, particularly those who are older and obese, it can be difficult or painful. So if your cat resists, give in to her better judgment.

Caring For Her Well-being

Your cat's eating habits can also provide important clues to her health and state of mind. For example, if she stops eating suddenly for just a short period of time, it could be a sign of a generalized infection. Starving herself as a cure, she is depriving the bacteria of the energy and minerals they need to survive. Because she is also weakened by lack of nourishment, she will rest and conserve her energy. Your cat may be so determined to rest and not eat that she will hiss, spit, or even try to scratch if you dare to approach her chosen lair. However, when your cat is ill, you need to deal with the root of the problem and have antibiotics administered by a vet.

If she eats less than normal over a long period of time and is losing weight, it may be an early indication of chronic illness, so it is wise to take her for a checkup. However, if her weight remains stable or increases and she seems happy and healthy but is out and about for long periods of time, it's a safe bet that you have a rival for her affection. It could be a person who is feeding her food she prefers. Try to stay tuned to the type of food your cat enjoys.

A Cat's Tale
Natural Acrobats

A cat's natural agility means they are among the most talented athletes in the animal kingdom. They can even stand up on their powerful back legs, using their tail to maintain their balance, to gain extra height. Cats often stand like this to catch an insect or butterfly, attempting to knock it down with a paw. As your pet grows older and less active, her reflexes slow, so her hunting instincts are less apparent.

How Your Cat Reads Your Body Language

Cats have a strong response to visual cues. And they are particularly interested in both other felines' and your facial expressions. Your cat reads in your countenance a complex mix of emotions and intentions, positive and negative, which determine how she is going to react.

It's well known that when a cat walks into a room full of people, she will usually approach the one person there who dislikes cats. But why? Is she psychic and behaving like this simply to be contrary? No—she is simply interpreting human behavior in cat terms. Cat lovers automatically stare at a cat who slinks seductively into a room, eyes wide, fur gleaming.

They can't help themselves. Cats, however, perceive this as a direct challenge to their presence rather than a display of interest or affection. People who are indifferent to cats simply don't look at them at all. This signals in cat language that they are benign, that they are well disposed to the newcomer, and would be very happy for her to approach. Almost immediately, your cat is on their lap!

Showing Her Your Feelings
When your cat begs, comes when called, or shows some other sign of responding to you so you want to praise her, bend down to her level. Let her see the emotions crossing your face and drink in their meaning. Communication is a two-way process—besides learning how to communicate effectively with your cat, you need to understand what she is saying. All cats have a large repertoire of facial and body expressions, which they use to communicate effectively with one another. They also convey enormous amounts of information through scent marking. Kittens and their mothers talk to one another constantly. They also have a wide range of distinct vocalizations,

Teach your children how to understand your cat's moods and emphasize that there will be times when the family pet wants to be stroked and others when she wants to be left alone.

which they use to convey very specific messages to each other and to us (see Chapter 3 for more information).

Cats are aware that humans have very little ability to communicate by scent, and a limited ability to use facial and body expressions effectively. Luckily, they realize early on that vocalization is an effective means of gaining their mother's attention; therefore cats understand the principle of communication by vocalization, and they put enormous effort into teaching us their language.

Listening To Your Cat

To understand what your cat is saying, really listen to her. Absorb the different vocalizations she makes at different times. "Meow" is never just meow when your cat is addressing you. Often it is a simple request to accomplish a task that she cannot perform without your help: Maybe she is saying, "Let me out!", or "Open the refrigerator and give me some smoked salmon now!" But it can also be a very important nugget of information about her physical or emotional well-being.

Mother cats can tell their kittens with vocalizations whether the supper they are bringing home is a mouse (never dangerous) or a rat (possibly lethal if it is only stunned and able to revive in the nest). If you pay close attention, your cat may be able to tell you that she much prefers cream to

Even young children like to play with cats, but make sure you are nearby to supervise to be sure that neither gets hurt.

chicken. She may also be able to tell you something else about how she is feeling.

It's all a matter of observation, and spending some time unraveling this fascinating mystery can only deepen your inter-species bond and reward you with extraordinary insight into your cat's world.

Kittens will soon adapt to their new home and rapidly come to trust you, but do not be surprised if your pet is nervous at first.

Sitting Comfortably

A person's size relative to that of a cat can act as an obvious barrier to good communication. It is important to lift your cat up and place her alongside you when you are sitting down so that she will feel closer to you. Not all cats are instinctive lap cats, and as they become older, cats often find it more uncomfortable to sleep this way, preferring to lie alongside people. Longhaired cats may feel uncomfortably hot, and rheumatic cats may find it painful, preferring to lie out alongside us instead. If your feline protests, let her go.

Getting In Touch

Stroking your pet can be another way of reinforcing your bond, as long as she is feeling relaxed and secure.

This silver tabby is rubbing against the leg of this stool just as she would against one of your legs, depositing her scent and laying claim to the territory.

Most cats let you stroke the tops of their heads, and if they are enjoying this attention, they purr and tilt their heads to one side, encouraging you to stroke under their chins or caress their silken ears. If your cat is lying on her side, stroke her flank gently and rhythmically. The more often you do this, the more she will enjoy it.

If she is feeling very relaxed, your cat may lie on her back, exposing her tummy. But does she want you to stroke it? Yes and no. In this position your cat is at her most vulnerable, but most dangerous. Her teeth and sharp claws are all available for attack. Differing emotions can war in her mind—she may savor the sensual feeling of having her tummy stroked, but even if she accepts this caress at first, she may move her hind legs up, and prepare to attack. One stroke too many and your cat may scratch your hand, or simply decide she has had enough and stroll archly away. Be guided by her responses, and over time your relationship will deepen.

Kittens often lash out with tiny paws or bite with milky white teeth when stroked. Often, this is because they really want to play—now where's that mouse on an elastic string? Kittens can be particularly playful before dinner, when they recognize the first stirrings of hunger. They are simply following an eternal hunting instinct, for it is play that allows a kitten to learn the skills she will need to hunt a mouse or deal with a rat.

The Scratching Post
Contact With Feral Cats

Kittens who are used to seeing people in their world but are never touched by them only tolerate us. Our presence does not make them nervous, but they remain aloof, disinterested in our attentions, and back away from expressions of physical affection.

Just like wild animals, feral felines—those who grow up exclusively with other cats—mature with an instinctive distrust of people that is irreversible. A cat feral from birth can never become your pet. She may accept offerings of food left in your yard, but she will never enter your home. She neither craves affection from us nor has any desire to bestow it. It's hard not to be tempted by the wild beauty of feral cats with their thick, colorful fur, but even if you hand-rear a feral kitten at home, the likelihood is that she will never be yours. Her only aim will be to escape your company.

Can't We All Get Along?

Our lives change constantly. We may meet a new partner, who comes with a cat or dog. A parent may die and leave us to look after their pet. The way we handle these situations in their early stages is critical.

**Introducing Stepcats:
Understanding The Rules**

Cats are territorial creatures, and they often object very strongly to newcomers—feline, canine, or human—invading their territory, at least at first. Put yourself in your cat's place: imagine a complete stranger suddenly appearing in your house, sitting on your favorite sofa, eating your chocolate, snoozing on your bed, and finishing off the milk. How annoying would that be? Wouldn't you do everything you could to eliminate this irksome invader? A cat feels this invasion strongly, and it's up to you

Introducing A New Cat Into Your Home

- Feed the cats in separate places.

- Make sure the newcomer has her own litter box in a place your cat does not normally visit—your cat may use her rival's litter box to establish it as her territory. The newcomer is driven away and forced to urinate and defecate elsewhere—which may be your bed, that lovely silk cushion you bought last week, the Ficus plant in the corner... (see the Cat Behavior A–Z, page 164)

- Don't play with either cat while the other is in the room—two cats chasing after one ball will cause conflict.

Dogs and cats can form a strong bond, especially if they grow up together, although at first they may be rather wary of each other—as shown by this kitten's uncertain reaction to her new companion.

to take the necessary steps to diffuse any conflict until all parties have settled down.

If you have introduced a second cat, both cats will initially be wary and may spend long hours stalking one another. In time, however, as long as you do not force them into one another's company, they will establish their own, unique way of living together. If your cat is an older female, she is likely to welcome a youthful, playful feline, adopting and mothering her. If the newcomer is the same age as your cat, the two may squabble at first and then become companions. Other personalities may simply live separate lives and carve out their own territories. Cats are individuals, and their relationships are multifaceted.

A New Dog In The Family

Introducing a dog into your household—although initially more problematic—is likely to develop into a harmonious relationship more quickly, because your cat won't feel so territorially threatened by a dog.

Initially the two may have a standoff. Cats and dogs have been known to stare at one another, utterly motionless for hours, until finally one makes a dash for the other or one simply becomes bored and wanders off. The dog may try to corner your cat who will probably seek sanctuary under the bed or on top of a cabinet. But in almost every case, after some initial skirmishes, the two settle down and become firm friends, even sleeping together. And the dog often takes his friendship seriously,

Older cats can be surprisingly trusting and patient with kittens, but allow them time for their own unique relationship to evolve rather than trying to force them together.

protecting your cat from rivals—driving invading felines from his new pal's territory.

When Your Cat Is Unfaithful

Sometimes, unintentionally, we fail to give our pet the attention she craves. We are busy, there is a deadline at work, or we are simply accustomed to her warm furry presence. We think nothing of it—but our cats are sensitive to this diminished affection and, if bored, seek it elsewhere.

Your cat may wander to another doorstep. Once there, she may meow pitifully, giving every appearance of being lost. Human hearts melt at the sight of this poor sad creature; arms and then refrigerators will open wide. Soon your cat is visiting this accommodating human on a daily basis—one day she may leave forever. Once you realize this is happening, it's time for action. Attach a message with your phone number to your cat's collar, and ask if anyone she is visiting could give you a call. If they do, explain your plight. Ask the well-meaning stranger if they would mind not feeding your cat. You miss her! And once she realizes home is the only place dinner is served, you hope she will return more often. If she does, it's up to you to make home so interesting she never feels the impulse to stray again.

Cat Custody Battles

Of course, sometimes it is human relationships that break down. Your partner may leave and want to take "their" cat, or dog, with them. It's hard at times like this to always think what's best for the animals in our lives, because we have such strong emotional bonds with them. But they are depending on you to make the wisest decisions you can for them and their future. And every situation is different.

If a dog and cat have been living together for years, with the cat curling up in the shelter of the dog's legs night after night, splitting them up is going to be a traumatic experience for both. Or opting for joint custody over a cat—shuttling her from place to place all the time—can be both deeply distressing and utterly unsettling for the cat.

But perhaps your cat never really did accept the overpowering newcomer and so will actually welcome their disappearance and the restoration of her territorial primacy. Only you can judge.

Cats are very patient creatures by nature, whether hunting or engaging in minor territorial disputes, like these two cats (opposite), staring very intently at each other. Ultimately, one will get up and wander away.

This cat (below) is in a playful mood and entreating you to give her some attention. Just be very careful that your cat's mischievous ways don't lead to your hand being seized between her front paws.

Caring For Your Cat Throughout The Seasons

Like all other creatures, cats who live in temperate areas of the world adjust their lives to the weather and to their changing circumstances. And we must also adapt to these changes.

There's plenty for a kitten to investigate and learn about outdoors. Don't be surprised if your cat hides away at first—it is just a sign of initial nervousness.

Spring

In spring your cat will shed her dense winter coat and will need frequent grooming—particularly if she is a longhair. As the weather becomes hotter, she will leave earlier in the day to stalk and play. She may climb onto that warm bench to nap blissfully in the sun while her body manufactures vitamin D—vital for health—through a biochemical process triggered by sunlight falling on her coat. But hours spent in the sun can, paradoxically, be unhealthy, particularly for cats with white fur and pink ears that are prone to sunburn and skin cancer.

If your cat has pale skin, buy her a special sunblock. You can massage that onto the tips of her ears to protect them from the harmful effects of ultra-violet light. Don't be tempted to use human sunblock, because it contains chemicals that can harm your pet.

Summer

Cats love to roam after dark; toms in particular can disappear during the summer, sometimes for days at a time. And your plaintive calls will mainly go unanswered because your cat has purely biological imperatives on his mind.

Neutered cats may roam less, but they, too, will feel the call of age-old instincts and long to patrol their territories and hunt for succulent rodents in the warm and inviting night. Your cat will return. But if you are worried for her safety—if you live near a busy road, for instance—try setting up a routine of tempting her home by rewarding her obedience with a succulent treat.

will also look for signs of any rodents in search of snug winter quarters.

Winter

In winter you will see much more of your comfort-loving cat, yet whatever the breed, your cat or kitten will enjoy venturing out into the snow. If the ground is frozen solid, your cat will be unable to dig in the earth, an important element in her toilet ritual. She may soil inside your home as a result, perhaps using your potted plants as a convenient substitute. It's time to buy a litter box!

Your cat will still hunt in winter, and this can be devastating for a bird population verging on starvation. Put a bell on her collar to warn birds when she is coming, and put out food for birds on cat-proof tables, which have a ring around them to prevent cats from climbing up.

By fall a young cat born in spring will have gained the confidence to patrol his territory, often being quite ready to drive off any intruder she encounters.

Fall

The look of breeds such as the Maine coon starts to change dramatically at this time of year as they begin to grow their longer winter coats. Even so, as the weather becomes cooler, cats will generally start to spend longer indoors again, where it will be warmer, and they will also be less inclined to wander at night.

Young cats often seek to improve their hunting skills by chasing after leaves blowing along the ground. They

Caring For Your Cat At Vacation Time

We all want to take time out to go on vacation, visit friends, explore exotic faraway lands, or simply chill out in the sun. But what about your cat?

Some cat owners decide the best option is to put their feline into a reliable well-run cat kennel, where she will be safe. Your cat, however, may have other ideas—particularly if you have done this before. Sensitive to changes in routine and the significance of an open suitcase, your crafty cat may simply decide to disappear. You then have two options: miss your flight or ask a friend to find your cat. The answer is to book her into the kennel a couple of days in advance so she has no idea of your true intentions.

Another option is to book a reliable pet-sitter to come and stay in your home. If you have more than one pet, this is an extremely cost-effective solution and your pet sitter can also water plants and take in the mail. Your

Comfortable surroundings will help your cat adapt to a temporary stay in a kennel. Check out the environment in advance to make sure you are happy.

cat will appreciate being in her own familiar surroundings, snoozing on her favorite cushion and stalking through your flower beds, and she can also entertain herself by wheedling extra treats out of this new obliging human!

If you're just going away for the weekend, it's fine to ask a neighbor to feed your cat, but for more extended periods of time, this could prove tricky. Your cat comes home not just for her food, but also for the companionship of her human family. And if that family's absent, your cat is likely to amuse herself elsewhere. There's always something to explore, or she will take time to find a warm spot in the sun, which is perfect for dozing. Neighbors can often be cajoled into letting her spend an hour or two on the sofa. But there's always the outside chance that your cat could fall ill or have a serious car accident and your neighbor might not realize anything is wrong—until she finds your cat's food untouched.

Of course, cats naturally miss the presence of their human families, but they don't pine in the way that a dog does, so try not to feel guilty about going away. If you are back home in two or three weeks, your feline companion will slip naturally back into your life. It will be just as if you had never been away.

As Your Cat Gets Older

How you treat your cat as she begins to age has a profound effect on her emotional and physical well-being. It's all too easy to miss the imperceptible changes that will lead to problems in the senior cat. There are cats that are old at 10, and those who are still youthful at 15. Although aging is genetically predetermined, your cat's environment has an overwhelming effect on how she ages mentally.

Keeping Her Brain Active

There's no need to take for granted the slowing of old age in your feline. What she needs is mental stimulation, and if she receives it constantly, she can remain alert and lively for the majority of her life.

Your cat was born to hunt; she is one of nature's supreme ambush predators. From kittenhood, if left with her mother, she is trained for the hunt. Her play with other cats, or with you, has only one goal—to ready her to slay her prey. Her reflexes are sharp, her eyesight acute, and her concentration awesome. Hunting is a demanding job guaranteed to keep your cat fit.

If a truly feral cat fails in the hunt, she will starve; wild predators must succeed or die. Because we offer our domestic cats food and shelter, they can live much longer than their feral counterparts—if your cat fails to catch a mouse, she doesn't risk starvation. Stiffness in her limbs gradually makes her prefer the sofa to the rigors of hunting. In her prime, a tom carved out his territory and defended it from all visitors. Now he is vulnerable to younger rivals seeking to claim their first territory and he may even be injured. This can make him reluctant to patrol his territory, stroll on the lawn, or even bask in the sun. He is also less stimulated, so his mental acuity declines.

But make a real effort to play with your cat and the rewards will be astonishing. When she is 15 or 16, she may not be able to leap as she did when she was five, but you can play less physically demanding games with her. A ball rolled across the floor will grab her attention just as well as a

The coloration of some cats, such as this colorpoint, does alter as they grow older, with darker shading often developing on their flanks. However, black cats do not turn gray.

As cats grow older, their level of activity declines. This begins from about seven years onward, but changes tend to be subtle and are not easily noticed, particularly at first.

The Scratching Post
Nutrition For Older Cats

A good diet helps stave off the physical effects of aging. "Senior" diets include antioxidants, which keep at bay free radicals that age the body, while other ingredients act as joint protectors against arthritis. Natural anti-inflammatories, such as nettle tablets, may help reduce damage and pain. Your vet will be able to prescribe a special diet if your cat starts to suffer from kidney or heart failure, suggesting foods to help ensure that your cat will enjoy a good quality of life with you for as long as possible.

tantalizing feather toy bouncing on a piece of elastic above her head. She may not be able to squeeze under the sofa to retrieve her ball as she gets older—but isn't that what you're there for? The important thing is to keep her active. This will not only improve her coordination but also her general level of fitness.

Her nutritional needs are just as important, because these alter with age. There is a real risk that your cat could start becoming overweight, so be sure not to overfeed her. Special senior diets have reduced calories to take account of the lower activity level of older cats. This also helps to protect your pet from potential health problems linked with obesity, such as diabetes mellitus. Being overweight can also worsen other underlying health problems, such as arthritis.

However, the day will dawn when your cat seems stiff on waking. Years of running, leaping, and jumping powered by her hind legs will finally begin to take their toll. Even then, do not give up playing games with your pet (see Chapter 3 for more on playtime). They will still help her to stay fit and aid coordination, helping her stay mentally alert. All you need to do is adjust her routines so the games are not too energetic, and take care not to overtire her.

Helping Her Groom

As her stiffness becomes general, your cat will find it hard to groom herself, and the amazing contortions and stretches she performed earlier will become difficult, and later even impossible. But felines are fastidious. They hate their thick, beautiful fur being dirty or unkempt.

Groom your cat frequently and with as much care as she would groom herself. Enjoy her pleasure and the reinforcement of the special bond that links you together. Some cats enjoy being gently massaged, and for the rheumatic senior it can bring pain relief, especially if performed with the right essential oils, (see Chapter 2 for information on massage).

Anticipating Her Needs

As jumping becomes more difficult for your cat and her eyesight becomes less acute, she may be reluctant to leap onto her favorite chair or your welcoming lap. Anticipate her needs

so she can live her life as usual. If she stares and meows loudly to attract your attention when you sit down, lift and place her on your lap and put her down when she asks. (Don't worry about leaving her on a sofa. She will find it easier to get down from there.) For her comfort, buy her a bean bag or velvet cushion. Put this in a place that catches the sun for most of the day, or by a radiator. Your cat will be drawn to this warm, safe haven, and it will become another one of her favorite places.

Your relationship with your cat develops and changes throughout her life. As she gets older, she will become more dependent on you, but in her feline heart she is still her wonderful, true self. In her dreams she still chases mice and scales big trees, and she still loves you, the person who has nurtured her from kittenhood to seniority.

And all she asks is that you love her in return.

Introducing a young kitten to an older cat may encourage your older companion to rediscover some of her youthful playfulness.

Touch And Healing

Although cats tend to be solitary by nature, they will form close bonds with people they know well. You may even meet a cat on the street who comes up to you with its tail held up and allows you to stroke its head as it winds around your legs. Cats differ significantly in their acceptance of this type of contact, however, depending in part on their early experience in life.

Soft To The Touch

If you watch two cats that have grown up together and have a strong bond, you will see they tend to lick around the head and face—often behind the ears—when they are grooming each other. This is why cats generally like to have this part of their body stroked; it is the way in which they reinforce the bonds between each other.

Grooming in this way also has a practical significance because your cat finds it impossible to clean this part of the body by using her own tongue. Her flexible body enables her to curl around and reach other areas without difficulty, even her back and tail.

The Benefits Of Stroking

One of the joys of sharing your life with a cat is that you can enjoy close contact with your pet by stroking her.

Studies have shown that this can actually be beneficial to your own health, helping to lower your blood pressure. In fact, cat owners generally tend to be less likely to fall ill than people without pets and will visit their doctor less frequently.

The texture of cat's fur does differ, and this may influence your choice of breed—especially if you are seeking a purebred companion. While Persians have long, luxurious coats, the fur of the sphynx is very different. However, these cats enjoy being stroked, even though they have little fur on their bodies. The rexes also tend to have

The long, fluffy fur of the Persian feels very soft to the touch. Its coat is longer than that of other breeds—individual hairs measure up to 5 in. (12.5 cm) in length.

The coat of short-haired cats, such as this blue tonkinese, is of a consistent length throughout the year, unlike that of their long-haired relatives.

unusual coat textures, while the fur of the rare American wirehaired breed resembles lamb's wool.

The Siamese and Orientals have a particularly sleek appearance because they have very little undercoat and a glossy top coat. This is partly why they need far less grooming than breeds such as the Norwegian forest cat, whose appearance can alter quite markedly, depending on the time of year. These cats grow a thick coat during winter, which is responsible for the prominent ruff of longer fur around the neck. Then in the spring, when much of the insulating undercoat is shed and the coat becomes less profuse for the summer, they lose this ruff. This is a reflection of their origins, having evolved under

How It Feels

The texture of a cat's fur varies significantly between breeds. This is a reflection of the proportions of different types of hair present in the coat. Here are some typical coat textures:

Coat texture	Breed
Soft	Siamese (see page 117) and Orientals (see page 122)
Firm	British shorthair (see page 98)
Plush and soft	Exotic (see page 120)
Short and silky	Cornish rex (see page 101) and Russian (see page 128)
Long and silky	Birman (see page 124) and Balinese (see page 117)
Feels like the skin of a peach	Sphynx (see page 104)
Feels like lamb's wool	American wirehair

natural conditions in areas where the winters are typically very cold, and the summers quite warm. Siamese—which originate from a region close to the equator—have no need for a thick winter coat.

Forming A Bond

Cats are highly affectionate animals, and it is very easy to form a bond with your pet, particularly if you have a kitten, simply by stroking and playing within her regularly. Cats can be remarkable creatures of habit, so if you always stroke your pet when you sit down, before long she will be seeking your attention whenever you sit. This logic applies also if you adopt an older cat that has been kept as a house pet elsewhere, particularly if you use the same name she has been used to hearing.

This cat (above right) is quite used to being held regularly so she is very comfortable in her owner's arms.

Your cat may often arch her body in this way when you run your hand down her back, or while being groomed.

It tends to be much more difficult to win the confidence of an older stray cat, but if she is not actually feral— born in the wild—then with a lot of patience and care it can be possible to persuade her to accept you in time.

How Your Cat Likes To Sit

An adult cat will probably have certain quirks as to how she will sit with you, whereas a kitten will be much more accommodating. Do not try to force an older cat to sit in a way that she finds uncomfortable, because she is unlikely to cooperate and it will simply weaken the bond between you. An older cat may, for example, be much more reluctant to roll over onto her back in your presence because this will make her feel vulnerable.

The Health Benefits Of Stroking

If you are out at work during the day, spend time with your cat when sitting down each evening. Cats can benefit significantly from being stroked and this will also allow you to examine your pet when she is relaxed. You will be able to see if her ears are dirty or if there is tear staining around her face.

Run your hands gently down each side of your cat's body and over her back to pick up on any slight swelling that may be hidden by the fur. This may be an early indicator of a health problem, such as a bite that is beginning to swell up into an abscess, or a skin tumor in an older individual. It is usually possible to distinguish between these two types of swelling: An abscess feels hot to the touch because it is the result of an infection, and it will grow rapidly in size over the course of a day or so. Tumors do not develop quickly, and they do not tend to cause a cat so much initial discomfort.

Checking For Fleas

Regularly stroking your cat can also help you detect other health problems, especially parasites that could affect you, too. Cats often suffer from fleas, especially during the summer months—although these parasites can often be a year-round problem. You are unlikely to see the fleas themselves, but you will notice the flea dirt when grooming your cat—it appears as small blackish specks in the coat.

To check that this is genuinely flea dirt and not just debris your cat has picked up, transfer some of the specks to a piece of damp facial tissue. If they dissolve and leave a reddish stain on the paper, this is a confirmation that your cat does have fleas. You may also notice that your cat is scratching herself more frequently, which can be another clue to the presence of these annoying parasites.

Noticing Ticks

If your cat ventures outside regularly, you may also notice ticks when you are grooming her—especially if you live in or near a very rural area.

Cats often scratch briefly on waking, but prolonged or repeated scratching is likely to indicate the presence of fleas in the coat.

The Scratching Post
Flea Collars

These used to be the preferred method for long-term flea control, but they are now less popular. They are not as effective as more recent methods and sometimes trigger skin problems themselves. Special collars impregnated with a natural remedy such as citrus oil, which does not kill fleas but deters them, are available in pet stores. However, most cats object to wearing collars of any kind, and even elastic collars can be dangerous, so it is better not to rely on them as a means of controlling fleas.

Wiping away tear staining on a Persian longhair. Cats usually accept being groomed very readily, but you may need to be patient with your pet at first.

If it is possible that your cat has ticks, be extra careful when combing her coat. Although a tick may be very tiny when it anchors onto your cat, its body will quickly become engorged with blood as it feeds. If you catch the tick with the comb, you could rupture its body, which may give the impression that your cat is injured. You are also likely to leave the tick's mouthparts embedded in your cat's skin, and this can easily develop into a local infection. This is one reason why it is always a good idea to stroke your cat thoroughly before you start to groom her—hopefully, you will pick up on any problems of this type with your hand and be able to look more closely before using the comb.

Ticks tend to be more of a problem in the summer than at other times of the year. They must be removed without delay because they can spread other diseases to your cat as they feed.

Cats Grooming Themselves

A cat will often spend long periods grooming herself during the day—especially after eating or exercise and before settling down to sleep.

You will notice that your pet follows a very precise ritual each time, particularly when cleaning her face. In spite of having a very agile body, a cat obviously cannot lick her own face. She cleans her front legs first with her tongue before starting to wipe her paws over her face.

She will then tend to move her foot in a circular direction down over her forehead, starting just in front of one of her ears. She will keep her head tilted to one side as she grooms this area, so that ultimately she has moved around the side of her face in

Treating Ticks

- Special sprays can persuade a tick to loosen its grip and fall off. However, this may be upsetting to your cat, particularly if she has a number of ticks clustered on her body.

- Alcohol dabbed onto these parasites close to the skin may be enough to loosen their grip.

- Petroleum jelly wiped over the rear of the tick's body will block its breathing apparatus and cause it to fall off.

- A number of flea treatments applied as a drop to the cat's skin are also effective against ticks. They should be used routinely in regions where ticks can spread serious illnesses, such as Lyme disease.

Cats are fastidious about grooming themselves, using their front paws to clean their faces.

The Power Of Fur

It is not just domestic cats that are susceptible to fur balls, they afflict other members of the cat family, too. If fur balls remain in the stomach, they can become impregnated with mineral salts and transform into stones. In Africa fur balls have been found in the stomachs of lions, and traditionally these were highly prized. They were often made into amulets and were believed to give the wearer great power that matched the lion itself.

a circular pattern, finally reaching behind her other ear.

Your cat will repeat this sequence using her other paw on the opposite side of her head. The eyes are the last part of her body she cleans. She can clean the rest of her coat directly by using her tongue and adjusting her position as necessary to reach her back and tail.

Fur Balls

A problem with grooming this way is that the rough surface of the tongue, which is caused by backward-pointing projections called papillae, will remove any loose hairs from the coat.

The cat then finds it very difficult to remove these hairs from her tongue, so they are likely to be swallowed. In time they will form a solid pad in the stomach, which is known either as a fur ball or a hairball. See page 166 for more information on fur balls and how to treat this problem.

Grooming Your Cat

The amount of grooming that your cat will need depends on your choice of breed; long-haired cats will need more grooming than their short-coated counterparts. The cat's age is another significant factor because young Persian kittens have much less profuse coats than adults. In spring, when they are molting, cats generally require more frequent grooming to remove their thick winter coat.

Nervous Cats

Cats can sometimes be nervous about grooming, and an older cat that you have adopted may not be used to this treatment. As with all new experiences, it is a good idea to accustom your cat to

Grooming Brushes

Rubber brushes

Slicker brush

Double-sided brush

Combs

Clipper

It is much easier to accustom a very young kitten to being groomed than to begin when she is an adult cat. Always be very gentle when grooming her coat.

A variety of grooming tools for cats, including different brushes and combs. The choice of equipment depends partly on the length of your cat's coat.

being groomed early in life so she will come to accept it as part of a regular routine. You are also less likely to encounter mats in the coat of a young long-haired cat.

When To Groom Your Cat

To groom your cat successfully, she will need to be relaxed, so start off by stroking her for a short time first. It is not a good idea to try grooming just before mealtime, because she will be hungry and much more interested in finding food.

The tools you need for grooming will differ to some extent, depending on your cat's coat. It is also important to be sure your cat is at a convenient height so you can groom her easily. You can use a table that is protected with newspaper or a thick blanket.

Grooming Short-haired Cats

Grooming a short-haired cat is usually very straightforward. Working with the lie of the fur, start from the back of the neck and comb toward the tail, as if you were stroking her. Work around the sides of the body, and when you reach the legs, try to groom them horizontally. Remove the loose fur from the comb as it accumulates between the teeth.

Cats particularly like being groomed with a rubber brush, which also acts as a skin tonic to improve circulation. You may notice that your cat pushes back against the brush as you rub her coat. Some cats will enjoy being

A Cat's Tale
Mutual Grooming

Cats groom each other for a number of reasons: besides maintaining the coat in good condition it has a social element. Cats who know one another well groom each other to reinforce their bond. This is why your cat may lick your hand when she is stroked—although some felines do this more than others. Do not encourage your cat to pull at the threads of your sweater though; this can lead to a behavior problem called wool-sucking (see page 184).

groomed so much that they lie down on their sides and may even roll over, which can make the process rather difficult!

Grooming Long-haired Cats

With a long-haired cat, use a comb or brush and start by grooming against the lie of the fur. This raises the hairs so you can strip out all the loose undercoat hair more effectively than

Kittens will instinctively groom themselves using a combination of tongue, teeth, and claws depending partly on which part of the body they are working on.

How To Groom

Routine brushing can shape the coat and give it a good gloss, but it is less effective than combing for removing loose hairs.

A slicker brush, which is square with numerous small metal teeth, should be used gently to break up mats in the coat.

Take particular care when grooming your cat's head near her eyes. A nervous feline may resent being touched here.

by just combing it down. Finish by brushing the coat. The tail can also be groomed in this way.

If your cat has a distinctive ruff, use a small fine-toothed comb around the face and work in the direction of the fur. Take great care to avoid your cat's eyes in case she suddenly decides to move.

Mats can develop very quickly in the coats of longhairs if they are not groomed daily. Severe mats may have to be cut out, but the fur will grow back.

Dealing With Mats

By grooming your cat regularly—which should be every day with a Persian longhair—you can prevent mats from forming in the coat. These can be extremely difficult to deal with if the undercoat has become severely matted together with the topcoat. If you simply try to comb your way through the mat, it is likely to be very painful for your pet and she is likely to resent it strongly—after all, it is just like having your hair pulled! One solution is to buy a special grooming comb with revolving teeth. These do not grab the hair in the same way as a comb with fixed teeth, so they can help to break a mat down gently by teasing it apart.

Pain-free Grooming

Rather than making the grooming experience unpleasant for your cat, the best thing to do may be to cut out matted areas of fur. This may prevent your cat from becoming nervous about grooming in the future, which would be far worse than temporarily losing a patch of fur.

Grooming Older Cats

As cats grow older, they become less mobile and cannot groom themselves as easily. Keep a close watch, especially on long-haired pets, to be sure that their rear end is kept very clean. You may need to clean this area and cut away any soiled fur to keep your cat healthy and free from infection.

The Scratching Post
Cats And Human Medication

Never be tempted to give your cat a human medication of any kind. Even basic human drugs such as aspirin and acetaminophen can have serious effects in cats because of their unusual metabolism.

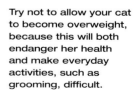

Helping A Cat With Arthritis

Cats can also suffer from painful arthritic joints as they become older, and this may affect the way you handle your pet. Be careful when lifting her. If you cause pain, she may attempt to scratch you. Be alert to what your cat is telling you. In the early stages she is likely to raise a front paw and perhaps hiss slightly as a sign of discomfort. The pain is likely to be most acute in her hip joints, so take extra care not to tuck her legs up tightly under her body when carrying her, thereby put pressure on her hips.

Consult your vet when you notice a problem, because there are ways to overcome joint problems, apart from painkillers. The pain of arthritis is caused by the cartilage wearing away and exposing the bone, which then grates as the joint moves. Supplements such as green mussel extract may be valuable. They act as chrondroprotectors and help to restore the cartilage.

Try not to allow your cat to become overweight, because this will both endanger her health and make everyday activities, such as grooming, difficult.

Bathing

Despite popular belief, many cats find water fascinating.

If your cat is already used to being both touched and carried, then she is less likely to resent being bathed. There seems to be a widespread view that cats actively dislike water, but many cats find it fascinating and will play with a dripping tap for hours, pawing at the water droplets as they fall. Outdoors their dense coat protects them against rain. Some species of wild cats live near water and may swim on occasion.

It is not often necessary to bathe a cat—if she comes in with muddy fur, let the mud dry and then brush it out of the coat. Old-fashioned flea treatments meant bathing your cat with an insecticidal shampoo to kill off these parasites, but this is now a thing of the past.

However, if the coat is soiled badly, it may need washing, and there are also medical conditions that may require the coat to be washed. Elderly incontinent cats, for example, may need their fur washed—especially if they have diarrhea.

Cats are always very curious as kittens, often using their paws rather like hands to touch objects gently.

Shampoo

Use a special feline shampoo to bathe your cat. If you have to remove an unusual substance—such as paint—from your cat's coat, be sure to seek advice from your vet. Cats like to lie under cars and may easily get oil on their coats, which must be removed without delay or your cat may lick it off and swallow it.

Some owners use a hair dryer to dry the coat, but most cats are very alarmed by the loud noise and air movement and will run away—often scratching more violently than when being bathed.

Before You Bathe Your Cat

When washing your cat, it will help to have someone assist you. It may be a good idea for both of you to wear gardening gloves, which will offer some protection if your cat becomes frightened and upset. Rather than trying to wash your cat outside, where she is more likely to run off and disappear, choose a room indoors with an impermeable floor, such as the kitchen or bathroom, and close the door. Prepare everything in advance and use a large bowl as a bath. Fill the base with tepid water—the idea is not to submerge your cat completely, but to use this water to create a lather with the shampoo. Try not to wet more of your pet's fur than necessary.

Step 1 Lift your pet carefully into the bath and reassure her—talk in a gentle voice to help her to overcome her fear. Try hard not to wet your cat's head, because this will probably cause her to struggle violently.

Step 2 Gently start to wet the area of fur that needs washing. Once the fur is wet, you can rub in a little shampoo to form the lather. It is very important to keep the shampoo out of her eyes.

Step 3 Keep a separate container of tepid water ready to rinse out the lather. Some medicated shampoos are not supposed to be rinsed out of the coat, so check the instructions carefully before you begin.

Step 4 Once you have washed and rinsed the affected area thoroughly, wrap your cat in an old towel and begin to dry her off. Do not let her go outdoors until her coat is completely dry, because she is likely to become chilled, especially if the weather is cold.

Bran Bath

It is not always necessary to bathe your cat with water. Breeders often prefer to give their cats a dry shampoo—or bran bath—to remove any excessive grease from the coat.

The bran is available at most pet shops or equestrian outlets because it is frequently used as a food for guinea pigs and horses. Spread it out

Cats keep their coats very clean. The patterning of short-haired cats stands out much more because the short, sleek coat improves the density of markings.

in an even layer on a flat tray and place it in the oven on a low heat for a few minutes to warm it up, then tip it carefully into a bowl.

Applying this to your cat's coat will be a messy process, so choose somewhere where it will be relatively easy to clean up afterward. Put down several sheets of old newspaper for your cat to stand on. Then simply rub the bran thoroughly into the coat, leave in place for a few minutes, and then give your cat a very thorough grooming to brush it out.

This can be an extremely time-consuming process, and unless it is done properly and very carefully, your cat may look as if she has developed a severe case of dandruff—particularly when pieces of bran are offset against a black coat!

A Cat's Tale
The Case Of The Van Cat

Developing in isolation can have a direct impact on a cat's way of life, as shown by the Van cat. Its natural homeland is in a remote area of eastern Turkey, adjoining Lake Van. It has evolved a very strange behavior, unlike that of any other breed of cat, because it loves to swim! Although it may catch fish while swimming in the lake, it is more likely that the cat's fondness for water is due to the region's intense summer heat.

Dealing With Stress

Repeated meowing or pacing back and forth while keeping low to the ground are clear signs that your cat is feeling nervous. This may be because a visitor has brought a dog or because of a significant disturbance in the cat's normal routine, such as builders in your home. Take extra care if major work is being done, because in a desire to seek out a quiet, safe refuge, your cat may venture under raised floorboards or behind cabinets and become trapped.

Frightening Weather

Thunderstorms frequently upset cats. It tends to be the noise rather than bright flashes of lightning that is the problem. Try to watch the weather forecast and keep your pet inside if a storm is imminent. If frightened, your cat may hide in the neighborhood and not return home for a couple of days, which can be a very worrying time.

Fireworks

The same advice applies for fireworks, so when celebrations are planned, make certain your cat is indoors for the night before darkness falls, and offer her a litter box, if necessary.

Keep her in a room with the curtains drawn to mask out the bright flashes of light, and play soothing music to mask the sound of the explosions.

You can see from this cat's body language that she is frightened. She may react aggressively if you try to pick her up.

Bach Flower Remedies

An English homeopath, Dr. Edward Bach, devised natural remedies in the 1920s and 1930s to regulate mood changes in his patients. He believed treating changes in the emotional state would prevent and overcome physical signs of illness. He formulated 38 remedies based on plants. They have become popular recently with pet owners—particularly people with cats, perhaps because cats show obvious mood changes.

A significant advantage of such remedies is that they do not

Ten Things That Stress Your Cat

If your cat is affected by any stressors listed below, pay attention to her behavior and try to spend more time showing affection and giving reassurance.

1. Thunderstorms
2. Fireworks
3. Moving to a new home
4. Visiting the vet
5. Going to a kennel
6. A new baby
7. Strangers in the home
8. A new puppy or dog
9. Renovation or building work indoors
10. Having medication

cause harm and can be administered directly into your cat's mouth, without touching the lips, or as a drop in food. One such treatment commonly used on cats is Rescue Remedy, which includes rock rose, to overcome fear and panic, and impatiens, for tension. Rescue Remedy is recommended for cats under stress, such as when a newcomer is added to the household, or after an accident or fight. It is available from specialist pharmacies.

Massage

Simply stroking your cat will help relax her muscles and improve muscle tone. You can also massage particular areas of your pet's body—perhaps because they are showing stiffness— but check how she reacts first to avoid an aggressive response. One of the most popular forms of massage for animals is a modification of the Feldenkrais method, which is used on people. It is particularly suitable for nervous cats since the repeated circular movements have a calming effect. They can be carried out for 15 minutes or so at a time.

Other techniques used on people can also be applied to cats. With effleurage you stroke rhythmically with an open hand along the body or down the hind legs. Pétrissage is an undulating technique that involves rolling the skin between the fingers and rubbing the muscle masses below.

Essential Oils

You can use essential oils in a massage for your pet, but never apply undiluted aromatherapy oils to the cat's skin, because they can be toxic. Dilute a drop of essential oil in about ½ tsp. (0.25 ml) of a carrier oil, such as sunflower or grapeseed, before applying. As an extra precaution, choose an area of the body that your cat finds difficult to reach with her tongue so she will not be able to lick the area easily—the back of the neck is a good location.

How to Stroke And Massage

Stroke the length of your cat's spine in a long, sweeping movement from head to tail.

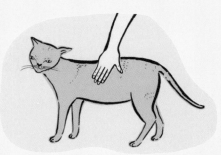

Massage with the pads of your fingers in little circles, moving in a clockwise direction.

Massage drops of the oil mixture into the skin for up to five minutes and repeat twice daily for four days. After each session wipe the oil off the skin in case your cat washes the area with her paw.

Galbanum And Myrrh

One particularly good oil for cats is galbanum, which aids healing and is useful for abscesses or fight wounds. Some cats—especially Orientals—suffer from chronic respiratory infections and sinusitis and may be helped by myrrh. Always check with your vet before using remedies of this type to be sure that they are suitable for your cat's condition.

Acupressure

This is a form of acupuncture, which relies on pressure instead of needles, but uses the body's meridians in the same way. Twelve pairs of meridians and two single ones are recognized, but there is no direct link between the location of the meridian and its effect on the body.

Studies have shown that meridians appear to be linked with electrical energy produced in the body. When pressure is applied, it can result in the release of natural painkillers, called endorphins, that may have a more direct effect on the healing process. A number of vets regularly use acupressure on their patients. Acupuncture is rarely used, because of the length of time the needle needs to be left in place in the skin—which may be up to 20 minutes.

Take Care!

If you use essential oils on your cat, there is a risk of an adverse reaction, even if they have been diluted correctly. This is a particular danger if your cat has an underlying medical condition, such as diabetes mellitus or epilepsy. Never use oils on cats that are, or could be, pregnant. Cats, because of their unusual metabolism, should not be treated with oils derived from plants containing phenols, such as aniseed, clove, and sweet phenol. Teatree oil can sometimes result in a skin irritation, and citrus oils should be avoided if your cat is going outside, because they can be affected by sunlight. A veterinary practice that offers complementary medicine will be able to advise you in more detail about what is suitable for your cat's condition.

Always handle your cat gently and make sure that there is no risk of dropping her.

Talk With Your Cat

Cats communicate in a variety of ways,
relying on their body language almost as
much as their vocalizations—particularly
when it comes to expressing their moods.
Here's how to interpret the signs she gives you
with her voice, body, and attitude. You'll soon
learn her special vocabulary; and will
be able to deal more effectively with
communication highs and lows.

Learn The Lingo

If you want to be in touch with your cat, you need to be able to understand what she is saying. Interestingly, domestic cats possess some highly distinct ways of communicating, which is not the case with their wild ancestors. It is believed that some sophistication has been derived from the different ways in which kittens communicate with their mothers.

When Kittens See And Hear

Newborn kittens are almost totally helpless at birth, because they are initially deaf and blind and unable to walk. A kitten that becomes separated from her littermates is able to crawl back because heat receptors on her face allow her to find the warmth generated by her littermates and their mother. Initially the mother will recognize her kittens by their scent only, but later she will be able to identify the individual calls of each kitten.

At about five days old the kitten's eyes start to open. It appears that kittens born to first-time mothers may open their eyes at an earlier stage than those in litters of more experienced queens. This may bring with it a survival advantage, despite the fact that they still are not very mobile at this point. There are also other considerations that affect when a kitten's eyes open, such as breed differences: larger, slower-maturing cats—such as Persians—may not be able to see until about 10 days. Bright surroundings may also delay this process.

A kitten's sense of hearing begins to develop just shortly after its eyes open. Up to this stage the kittens may seem rather unresponsive, but from now on they will be able to hear your voice and will start responding to the sounds around them. At three weeks kittens become mobile and will then rapidly begin to investigate their surroundings.

Cats not only depend on sound to communicate, but also rely significantly on both body language and scent.

The Scratching Post
The Cat's Love Call

It can sometimes be difficult to distinguish mating calls from caterwauling, especially because mating in cats is an aggressive act. Queens tend to screech even more loudly than during a fight when the tom withdraws his barbed penis from her body. The duration of the call is therefore often shorter, too.

Communicating With A Deaf Cat

Cats are generally far less afflicted with inherited and congenital problems than dogs; probably the most serious widespread problem that can crop up is congenital deafness in blue-eyed white cats. A deaf cat can adapt quite well to the disability, although it is more difficult to communicate with your pet if you cannot train her to recognize her name. However, you may be able to develop a sign language of sorts, beckoning your cat to come to you and tapping the sofa with your hand if you want her to jump up alongside you, for instance. It is important to think carefully before letting a deaf cat out to roam, because she will not be able to pick up the sounds of nearby traffic, which may have fatal consequences. There is also a risk that your cat could be caught unawares by a dog or even by another cat in the vicinity, and then she could be injured in a confrontation.

Young cats are often instinctively more playful than adults, because this is an ideal way for them to investigate and learn about their world.

What Is Your Cat Saying?

Cats have different dialects, and their vocalizations vary from country to country (in the same way as an East African parrot has a different accent to a West African parrot).

The sounds made by cats do differ significantly from breed to breed, in terms of emphasis and tone, similar to regional dialects, although their basic vocabulary is the same. Some breeds, such as Siamese, are instinctively more vocal than others, compared with a breed such as the Russian blue, which has a reputation for being a very quiet cat. Almost certainly within any group of cats, individuals will be able to recognize each other on the basis of their distinct vocalizations.

Even young kittens will purr, but be aware that it is not always a sign that all is well.

Purring

Purring is probably the most distinctive sound associated with cats, but it is unclear not only how this sound is made but also its exact meaning. Although purring is generally considered to be a sign of contentment, cats that are in serious pain may also purr, as well as very sick felines, so it is not always safe to assume that purring is a sign of happiness or good health.

Kittens can purr when just a week old, even before their eyes are open. This helps the family group to keep in touch—even in darkness, when the queen is suckling her offspring—because the mother will be able to hear her babies.

The sound of purring is also quiet, so predators would not be alerted to the presence of the queen and her offspring if they were in the wild. Purring also appears to be important for bonding in later life, with two cats that have grown up together purring readily in each other's company. The sound also reinforces the bond between a cat and her owner. It may sometimes be used as a means of calming a potentially aggressive situation, with the weaker feline responding to the threat from another cat by purring as well as adopting a docile pose.

Cats are able to purr with their mouth closed, while the sound itself is a double note. A cat may sometimes be purring even though the sound is not audible. You can detect the purring notes by placing a finger gently around the underside of the throat to pick up the vibration, which is likely to gain in intensity as you pay greater attention to your pet.

Purring may seem to be a fairly constant sound, but in reality, if you watch your cat's chest closely, you are likely to spot a short time lapse between when your cat breathes in and when she breathes out.

A Cat's Tale
How Your Cat Purrs

There are several theories to explain how a cat is able to make a purring sound. One suggests it has to do with the two folds in the cat's larynx. The first fold is the true vocal chords; the second, often described as false vocal chords, may be responsible for the purring sound.

Another theory involves the circulatory system. The blood returning to the heart travels along the collecting vein known as the posterior vena cava. It has been suggested that purring could be related to the turbulence from blood passing through the relatively thin wall of this blood vessel as it nears the heart. The sound of this may then reverberate from the chest up to the head.

Meowing

The other sound associated with domestic cats is meowing; this is made similar to the manner in which we speak. It is achieved through the larynx, or voice box, which is located at the back of the throat at the top of the trachea, and through which air flows back and forth to the lungs.

A cat can communicate by movements of its tail—and these may sometimes attract the attention of a kitten!

The vibration of the vocal chords consequently triggers the familiar meowing sound.

Hunting Sounds

Sometimes, if your cat is outdoors, you may suddenly hear an unusual clicking sound that is not loud but is quite determined. You are also likely to notice that the cat has dropped low to the ground, moving slowly forward with her tail held horizontal. This indicates that she is stalking prey. Mothers may use this very distinctive call to indicate to their offspring that they need to remain quiet at this stage so they won't scarce off the prey. Female wildcats often have a much lower success rate in catching prey when they have their kittens with them.

Caterwauling

Some calls that cats make can be quite alarming, particularly when they are about to fight. This often takes place at night, giving these sounds a ghostly air. These calls have become known as caterwauling.

The Scratching Post
A Lion's Roar

Only small cats in the family Felidae are able to purr, unlike the larger members, such as the lion, which vocalize by roaring. The sounds uttered by cats vary in intensity, with the roar of the lion being the loudest sound made by any member of the family. It is equivalent to 114 decibels—comparable to the noise of a car horn. Smaller cats are not able to make such loud sounds because they have a bony hyoid apparatus, which anchors the larynx in place, rather than the looser arrangement of cartilage that is a feature of bigger cats. They also have a smaller chest and, therefore, a smaller lung capacity.

Unlike meowing, for example, the shrieks and wailing sounds are long lasting, and their intensity increases as the risk of actual conflict intensifies. Once the conflict begins, there is likely to be screeching, which is clearly the sound of an animal in pain. However, this call has another function; it is aimed at shocking the other cat into letting go, allowing the underdog either to strike back or retreat rapidly.

The intensity of the sound made by a cat can be just as significant in meaning as the sound itself. Loud, more intense vocalizations often serve as a warning.

A Cat's Vocabulary

The vocalizations that cats make are influenced by a variety of factors, including their age, mood, and breed. It is not just the calls themselves that are significant for communication purposes, but also their intensity. If you ignore your cat when she wants attention, she is likely to react by calling more frequently and loudly.

Mewing
Young kittens are able to make a plaintive mewing sound when they are hungry or have lost touch with their mother or littermates. This is a distress call, intended to draw the female cat to her offspring, and it grows in both intensity and frequency if it is not answered quickly.

Murmurs
Older cats can express themselves by a much wider variety of vocalizations, including a series of murmurs when they are relaxed. These are often audible if you are stroking your pet, who is curled up alongside you. The cat barely opens her mouth when uttering these sounds.

Meow
The more assertive "meow" is made when an adult cat is seeking attention. Your pet may want food, is hoping to be allowed into another part of the home, or simply desires attention from you. Meowing is usually accompanied by body language indicative of what is on your pet's mind, whether curling around your legs hoping to be fed, or standing by a door, wanting to be let through to the other side. If ignored, your cat may persist in meowing for some time, with the sound intensifying as well. Certain breeds, such as the Orientals, naturally tend to have louder voices than others.

Meows are relatively brief calls, with the cat opening and closing her mouth clearly when making the

When a cat is seeking to communicate, she does not draw her lips back to expose her long canine teeth, as she does when she is in an aggressive mood.

sound, and they are often called vowel sounds for this reason. Sometimes, however, you may notice that your cat opens her mouth apparently intending to make a sound but seems to be struck dumb. This is probably a way of reinforcing meowing notes without becoming too assertive, and recognizing the dominance of the owner. Your cat now believes she has your attention.

Long Meow

In contrast, a more tense vocalization is likely to be evident when cats are communicating with each other. In this case the cat's mouth tends to remain open, with the lips drawn back slightly to show the long, pointed canines. The calls themselves may not be particularly loud or aggressive, however, especially if the cats know each other well. These sounds must be interpreted along with your pet's body language, to provide a clear indication of her mood.

Yowl

In aggressive encounters the pitch of the cat's vocalizations changes, becoming more intense and determined if the adversary will not back down. The purpose of these calls is simply to intimidate, and they are made as a direct threat to the other cat—or even dog or another animal— that is menacing it. As the calls become louder, the cat may also begin spitting as she hisses, which is a prelude to launching into an attack.

Cats often look up at us when they vocalize because they are instinctively watching to see how we are reacting—it's rather like having a conversation.

Body Language

Besides vocalization, cats depend on body language to communicate, so you need to be able to read the signs to have a clear indication of what your cat is saying. Facial features, body posture, tail movements, the shape of the pupils, and even the position of the whiskers are all important indicators of your cat's mood.

What Your Cat's Posture Means

When relaxed, a cat will lie with her ears held in an upright position with her whiskers hanging down each side of her face, and her front feet folded in the direction of her body. The eyes are likely to be partially closed, with the pupils usually oval in shape. She may be purring and will raise her head and utter a friendly murmuring note if you stroke her head. Or she may simply curl up into a ball and fall asleep. Subsequently, particularly in a warm environment, she is likely to roll over and stretch out.

Cats will also roll over onto their backs when relaxed. This is a sign of trust, because in this position a cat will be very vulnerable. Even so, not all cats like being stroked on their bellies. They are more likely to allow you to stroke the chest area rather than the abdomen. If they dislike this experience, they will kick out with their hind legs as a deterrent.

As shown by her body language, with her tail carried high over the back, this particular cat (above right) is both relaxed and confident.

Your cat will like to jump up alongside you onto a sofa, often climbing onto the arm to achieve direct eye contact.

How a Cat Says Hello

Cats will normally approach other cats head-on if they know them well, allowing them to rub the sides of their face against their own as a greeting. A cat usually greets a familiar person by attempting to stand briefly on her hind legs as a way of coming closer to the person's face. If the person sits down, the cat will almost immediately leap up alongside. A mother cat who is returning to her kittens will lower her head, allowing her kittens to rub against the underside of her jaws.

Scent Marking And Communication

At times your cat will pursue you, entwining herself around your legs. This is obviously an effective way of attracting your attention, which your cat quickly learned as a kitten, but it also serves another purpose. Such behavior is a reflection of the solitary yet territorial nature of cats, which means they need to be

A Cat's Tale
Territorial Marking

There are other clues to your cat's presence outdoors that you may not be aware of unless you observe your pet closely. Many cats have a favorite scratching area—a fence post or the trunk of a tree or bush—that they use regularly to keep their claws sharp. The marks left behind also indicate to other cats in the area that this territory is occupied. There will be a scent left here, too, because sweat glands between the toes enable cats to deposit their own individual scent as they scratch the wood. The clues may escape us, but cats are very aware of other cats nearby. For cats this is important, because unexpected encounters can lead to fighting.

Kittens soon come to recognize the scent of their mother, which is transferred to them when she is grooming her litter.

These two cats are rather wary of each other, but the one on the right appears to be more assertive.

able to communicate with each other over long distances. They have special scent glands on their body for this purpose, so by rubbing herself on your legs, your cat is depositing her scent. If you subsequently visit a

The Scratching Post
Fighting Injuries

Injuries sustained in a fight may seem relatively superficial, perhaps comprising just a single bite. However, this one bite may create an abscess within a few days or could even necessitate the amputation of a leg if a joint was damaged. Cats have bacteria present within their mouths that are injected deep into the opponent's tissue when they bite. The flesh above seals over afterward, creating ideal conditions for an infection to develop within the body.

friend who also has a cat, you may notice that she will be attracted to this area of your clothing, sniffing here to investigate your pet's scent.

Your cat will not only confine herself to depositing its scent on your

clothing, she will also behave in a similar fashion toward furniture, such as the legs of tables or chairs, always rubbing herself at the same height. Cats do this outdoors as well, depositing their scent on fence posts or other prominent areas, which cats can sniff as they pass. They will do this repeatedly because rain will wash away the odor. We cannot smell this particular scent—unlike the pungent urine of tomcats, which is a more noticeable territorial marker, particularly if there is another male cat in the neighborhood. Queens will tend to rely far less on their urine for scent-marking purposes, although it will draw nearby tomcats to them when they are ready to mate, because of the presence of chemical messengers known as pheromones.

Facing Threat
When a cat is wary, she will tend to keep her body very low, flattening her

ears and drawing back her whiskers along the sides of her face. At this point the cat may be relatively quiet, but if she finds herself cornered, her behavior will change and she will become more assertive, trying to intimidate the other cat. She will stand up as tall as possible, using her size to intimidate, with her ears flattened but pulled back so if a fight ensues, they will not easily be seized and injured by the other cat. The whiskers in this case are raised, as well as the fur along the cat's back—another means of trying to increase her height to deter her rival from attacking.

Vocalizations also play their part at this stage, with calls being used to intimidate. Usually the encounter is brief and the weaker feline will run off, pursued for a short distance by her opponent.

Backing Off

Because they are predators, cats are equipped with very sharp teeth and claws, so even the victor could be badly injured in a fight. When confronting an opponent, cats go through a series of actions to prevent conflict. For example, they tend to turn partly sideways toward the would-be opponent, which gives the option of running or fighting.

A cat will always try to position herself when threatened so that she has an escape route, rather than risk becoming trapped.

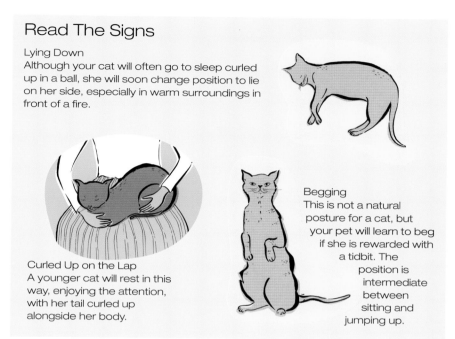

Read The Signs

Lying Down
Although your cat will often go to sleep curled up in a ball, she will soon change position to lie on her side, especially in warm surroundings in front of a fire.

Curled Up on the Lap
A younger cat will rest in this way, enjoying the attention, with her tail curled up alongside her body.

Begging
This is not a natural posture for a cat, but your pet will learn to beg if she is rewarded with a tidbit. The position is intermediate between sitting and jumping up.

This tabby is displaying very obvious signs of nervousness, with ears flattened on the sides of her head and her tail carried low as she crouches down close to the ground.

You can tell a lot about your cat's mood from her body posture. Based on the position of her ears and tail, this feline (above right) is rather nervous.

A cat's eyes (below) possess an almost hypnotic quality when seen close-up and can vary in color from amber to green through to shades of blue—depending partly on the breed and also the individual cat.

Telling Her Tail

It is not just facial features that help to indicate a cat's mood, her tail is also significant. When at rest, the tail is usually curled up alongside the body. If a cat is alert and trying to attract your attention—seeking food, for example—she is likely to raise her tail and hold it vertically. When a cat is angry, she will lower her tail and move it from side to side, the movements increasing in intensity as she becomes more annoyed. When hunting, the tail is kept low and held out behind the body, quivering slightly at the tip—which may indicate concentration before the cat pounces.

Look Into Her Eyes

The shape of the cat's pupils can alter quite dramatically, depending not only on the lighting conditions but also on the cat's mood. This is an aspect of body language that a cat cannot control instinctively, since it is mediated through the autonomic nervous system, which also controls those other parts of her body that may be

involved in a conflict situation, such as her heart rate.

A cat that is very scared will have circular pupils, which effectively mask much of the color of her eyes. This also happens at night when the muscles of the iris are constricted to allow as much of the available light into the cat's eyes as possible. When a cat is angry, her pupils contract to a narrow slit-like shape. This also occurs in bright daylight to shut out much of the light and prevent her from being blinded by sunlight.

Watch How She Uses Her Whiskers

Cats also use their whiskers in order to communicate. The whiskers are significantly thickened and modified hairs that possess a vital sensory function. For example, they enable cats to determine whether they can squeeze through a gap in a fence. The hairs on the sides of the face are the most evident, being split into four rows of three, with the top two rows able to move independently of the bottom two.

The cat's whiskers not only assist the cat in finding her way around in the dark but also aid her hunting ability, detecting issues such as wind direction. Cats with damaged whiskers—which are fairly common in rex breeds because of the changes in the structure of the hair associated with these mutations—find it more difficult to kill prey effectively in the dark. The whiskers also impart

What Her Pupils Say

Muscles in the eye control the diameter of the pupil, through which light passes to the retina at the back of the eye.

A cat's pupils reduce to a very narrow, slit-like shape in bright light or if she is badly frightened.

information that guides the cat to the exact position of her prey. When you are playing with your cat, she may use her whiskers as she does when she is hunting, chasing a toy almost without stopping, having assessed that it can slip easily through a gap in furniture. Cats can move their whiskers freely, holding them against the face when sniffing, or extending them forward to estimate distance or direction.

Communication Through Play

Play is a good way of developing communication between you and your pet, and this is something that you should be able to do either in the home or outside. Young cats particularly are very playful by nature—in the wild, littermates play with each other as a way of developing their coordination.

Which Toys To Choose

There are a number of toys that you can purchase for your pet, and your choice will depend on the age and agility of your cat. Some toys are saturated with catnip oil, derived from catmint (*Nepeta mussinii*; see the feature box, right). This can have a strange effect on cats, with many felines attracted to the herb,

particularly in its fresh state. Catmint is easy to cultivate in a garden, since it does not require special care. Cats that sniff and bite the leaves, or even simply rub against the plant, will later roll about on the ground, appearing relaxed and content. This is similar to the behavior of a queen when she is in estrus and therefore ready to mate.

Cats can display individual preferences when it comes to toys, and these can be influenced by your pet's early experiences at home with you. A simple ball that your cat can chase over the floor and play with in your absence is often popular. Wind-up moving toys will need you to be

Playing with your cat helps to build a bond between you, but your cat will prefer some toys to others.

present, however. Feathers on sticks can often encourage cats to sit up and play, but remember never to tease a cat when playing with her. For her to enjoy playing, a cat should always be allowed to have direct contact with her toy, rather than keeping the object well out of reach. Toys can also be incorporated into cat gyms, which provide an additional opportunity for cats to climb safely anywhere within the home.

Outdoor Play

Outdoors, cats may pounce on leaves that are blowing around in the wind or chase after a small ball, attracted primarily by movement. Their natural

The Scratching Post
Catnip: The Feline Happy Herb

Cats' attraction to catnip is unclear, but it is believed to be related to a chemical called nepetalactone, which is present in the plant catmint, from which catnip is derived. It has been suggested that nepetalactone is a sexual stimulant, but both neutered and intact cats respond to it, as do cats of both sexes.

What seems more likely is that the catmint induces a temporary state of relaxed euphoria, which lasts about 10 minutes. Although even large wildcats, such as tigers, may be affected by catnip in this way, it seems that young kittens under eight weeks old are more apt to avoid it. Most cats become susceptible to the effects of catnip only after the age of three months. What determines sensitivity is unclear, since not even all members of the same litter will be affected. Valerian (*Valeriana officinalis*), although not as potent, causes similar symptoms. Conversely, there are some plants cats tend to avoid, such as rue (*Ruta graveolens*), an herb that has been used since Roman times to dissuade cats from digging in flower beds.

curiosity can lead to problems, however, because they will pursue insects such as bees and wasps. This is part of the kitten's learning process; once they have been stung, most cats remember to avoid such insects.

Indoor toys often emulate the insects, animals, and colors of nature, although it is probably the movement of wind-up toys or a scent of catnip oil that attracts the cat.

Cats probably do not associate the appearance of a toy mouse with their natural prey.

Communication Breakdowns

Always be alert to the possibility of communication problems developing, especially with a recently acquired older cat, whose background may be unknown. Bear in mind that a cat that is frightened needs reassurance, but she may also lash out at you in fear, so she will need to be handled with great caution.

A Cat's Tale
Child's Play

Young children can easily provoke a cat into scratching or biting by playing too roughly, so supervise until they are old enough to treat your pet with respect.

When you are playing with your cat, do not allow her to bite or scratch in play, because this will teach her that such behavior is acceptable.

Cats will always try to position themselves with an escape route if threatened. The side-on approach may also make the cat look bigger.

Coaxing a Frightened Cat

If you can train your cat to respond to your calls, you will be able to coax her out of danger. This can be helpful in scenarios such as the cat-up-the-tree, for instance. Cats may find themselves in this situation when they need to escape a dog in pursuit. To seek shelter, they scamper up the trunk of a tree but then will find themselves in unfamiliar territory. Although cats can use their claws to effectively run up a tree, they have to clamber down backward, and most are afraid to do so. If you have developed a strong bond with your cat, you may be able to provide the encouragement she needs in order to lure her down and avoid calling the fire department.

Cats Who Hide

There will be times when the cat's solitary nature wins over her desire to be companionable with you. Do not try to force your cat to sit with you if she clearly does not want to settle down and sit on your lap. This behavior is especially common in older cats, simply because their

bodies are less flexible as they grow older and this in turn makes it much less comfortable to sit on you. Your pet is likely to indicate this by preferring instead to rest contentedly alongside you.

Dealing With Aggression Toward You

If your cat is seriously distressed or frightened, then she is likely to react aggressively, especially if you ignored the warning signs. Pain is probably the most common cause of cats striking unexpectedly at their owners. Should you fail to realize this, then your cat will scratch and may even bite you to stop you from hurting her.

Dealing With Reactions To Other Animals

Although cats tend to be much more solitary by nature than dogs, they can develop a close rapport not just with their owners, but also with other animals living in the home. However, they can also react very badly to other animals, either by becoming very aggressive or by hiding from them.

Cats And Cats

In the case of other cats, it is often very difficult to predict how two cats will take to each other, unless you start out with littermates or keep a kitten born to a female you already have. There is also a strong possibility that two kittens introduced to the home at the same stage will settle well together, even if they are not of the same breed. The hardest situation will be cases in which you already have one cat and decide to introduce another to the home. If your existing pet is a spayed female, she will be far more amenable to a newcomer than a cat that has not been neutered.

When you allow the cats to meet for the first time, do not immediately put them together because this will most likely lead to a violent reaction. Instead, allow them to meet on their own terms.

Domestic cats may be less quarrelsome than their wildcat ancestors, since maintaining a territory is no longer vital to obtain sufficient food for survival.

Although this may be accompanied by some wary hissing as they stalk around each other, this is far less likely to result in displays of outright aggression. Stay in the background, and only intervene if fighting seems inevitable. Do not close the door to the room, because there will be no simple escape route if the newcomer is unexpectedly attacked by your established pet.

Reassert your existing cat's dominance by not changing her routine; the newcomer will not be affected, but simply have to adapt to the existing state of affairs. Feed your new cat separately at first, which will both allow you to check that she is eating properly and ensure that the risk of conflict over food is reduced.

In time you may find that your cats become more friendly toward each other, which may take a couple of months or longer. Unfortunately, in some cases, this simply does not happen. The cats may not persistently fight; but they will simply avoid contact with each other at every opportunity.

Cats And Dogs

In spite of their popular image as rivals, cats and dogs can get along well and may even develop a close bond. This is especially true if you acquire a puppy and kitten at the same time.

Introducing a puppy to a home where there is already a cat is also likely to be reasonably straightforward and trouble-free, because cats do not regard the introduction of a dog as a challenge to their status. A puppy will learn to be respectful to a cat in much the same way that it will learn its place in the pack hierarchy. This is a key difference between cats and dogs, because dogs are social by nature. Some breeds, such as the Abyssinian, have a particular reputation for living well alongside dogs.

Cats And Puppies

A cat can often be surprisingly tolerant of the attention of a young puppy, although if things become too frenetic, the cat may hiss and even warn the puppy by unsheathing her claws. This may sometimes create a scratch, but generally a cat will not bite her companion and the puppy

Unlikely friendships may develop between dogs and cats—although some breeds of dog, such as this golden retriever, are more tolerant than others.

soon learns acceptable boundaries. Supervise their play during the early stages, simply because there is a risk that your cat could scratch your dog's eye, which is potentially serious, or a large dog might inadvertently injure a cat by rolling over her body.

Kittens And Dogs

It may be more difficult to introduce a young kitten when there is already an older dog present. Keep a close watch on them at first in case your dog chases and grabs the cat. The risk of this is higher in certain breeds, such as terriers and some hounds, which naturally hunt a variety of small game.

Cats And Small Animals

There may be other pets in your home that represent the cat's natural prey, such as hamsters, mice, and small birds. Despite stories about cats striking up a close relationship with such pets, the cat's innate hunting instincts leaves these creatures at serious risk of attack. It is therefore very important to keep other small pets in a part of the house from which your cat is excluded. You cannot watch your cat constantly, and the mere presence of a potential predator is likely to cause great distress to small mammals or birds, especially if your cat persists in trying to reach them.

Unfortunately, it is not always safe to allow your cat to roam freely, but you can train a young kitten to exercise on a harness attached to a leash, which will prevent her from running off.

If your cat manages to catch another pet, deal with the injury immediately. Even if the bite does not appear serious, the cat's mouth has bacteria that are likely to be introduced into the other animal's body by the teeth, triggering the development of a possible fatal infection. Clean out the wound at once and always seek veterinary advice, because antibiotics may be advisable.

The Scratching Post
Hunting At Home

Pet birds are especially vulnerable to cats when they are out of their quarters, simply because their flight will certainly attract attention. Domestic cats will hunt potential prey irrespective of whether or not they are hungry. In the wild, cats often kill more than they can eat at a single meal and will try to conceal the surplus for later—a behavior that is known to zoologists as caching.

Protecting Garden Birds

Cats will most likely pursue wild birds in the spring, when they are nesting and more vulnerable to being caught. Young birds represent relatively easy targets once they leave the nest. Design your garden carefully to make it more difficult for your cat to reach nesting sites or feeders, and position nest boxes out of your cat's reach—on the side of the building, for example. Pick a spot above a flowerbed with plenty of shrubs because most young birds leave the nest before they are able to fly well; if they flutter down into an area with no cover, they are

Do not assume your cat has lost the keen hunting instincts of her ancestors. Cats can rapidly revert to a free-living lifestyle.

vulnerable to predators. Protect birds that build open, cup-shaped nests in trees by attaching a wire framework around the base of the tree. This will make it much harder for a cat to reach the nest, because she will not be able to anchor her claws in the bark to climb. Landscape these wire hoops into the garden by training fast-growing climbing plants to twirl and entwine up them.

Aviaries can be protected with an ultrasonic device that emits high-frequency sounds inaudible to our ears but can be clearly heard by cats, deterring them from entering this area of the garden.

Positioning Bird Tables

Cats are ambush predators, so they are adept at hunting birds when they are feeding around a bird table. Position your bird table out in the open with good visibility all around. Make sure there is a clear line of flight down to and away from this feeding station so the birds will feel secure. Suspend hanging feeders well below tree branches so there is no risk of a cat catching the bird from above as it flies in to feed. If your cat still manages to catch a bird and you retrieve it alive, take it to a local animal hospital for treatment.

Protecting Fish In Ponds

In temperate areas fish in garden ponds are especially vulnerable to cats in early spring when the water temperature is still relatively cold and

the fish are sluggish. They will also be more conspicuous at this time of year because aquatic vegetation dies back and the water is clear due to the lack of microscopic algae.

Cats are also likely to be attracted to a pond in early summer, when the fish are starting to spawn. Cover the pond with a net at these times, or place a fence made up of wire around the edge to keep the cat away. If a fish is caught, it may simply be left on the ground rather than being eaten, so if you discover it in time, you may be able to save its life. Quickly transfer the fish to an aquarium filled with

Fish in a garden pond are not entirely safe from cats, although most cats prefer to drink the water rather than trying to catch the pond's occupants.

Farm cats tend to make the most effective hunters, since kittens are taken on hunting trips by their mother. She will also bring back prey so they can learn to kill.

alert or responsive as birds; a bell on the cat's collar will not provide an effective warning. The best protection is to screen off the garden near the pond. Leave the grass around the pond uncut once the tadpoles have become frogs, to provide more cover as they emerge from the water.

Toads And Your Cat

Conversely, your cat is at greater risk from the toad than the other way around. Toads have large swollen areas on the back of the head, called parotid glands, as well as other less evident glands on the skin. These combine to produce toxins over the surface of the amphibian's skin that will lead to great discomfort if your cat catches a toad in her mouth. Almost instantly these toxins produce intense irritation, causing the cat to start foaming at the mouth, usually followed by a period of repeated vomiting. Encounters with toads are most common in warmer weather, typically around spawning time or after a period of rain has drawn amphibians from their hiding places.

The precise impact on the cat depends on the species of toad. The most deadly is the giant or marine toad (*Bufo marinus*), a native of Central and South America but introduced into various countries, including various southern U.S. states and parts of Australia. If your cat comes home distressed, displaying symptoms of toad poisoning, rinse out her mouth to flush the toxin out

dechlorinated water, changing this as needed to reduce the risk of a fungal infection, and only return it to the pond when it has fully recovered, with any obvious injury already healed.

Frogs And Toads

Some cats may hunt other pond creatures, from insects to amphibians. Frogs are very vulnerable at spawning time because they congregate in the water in large groups. The female will be laden with spawn, making her less mobile, and may also have a male frog clasped to her back. Even minor damage to a frog's skin is likely to be fatal, and it is difficult to protect amphibians because they are not as

before more can be absorbed into the body. In areas where marine toads are present, seek immediate veterinary help. Although there is no specific antidote, various drugs can counter the venom, which may otherwise prove deadly.

Flying Insects

Colorful flying insects such as butterflies and bees represent an irresistible challenge to cats. Kittens, with their alert, playful natures, are most likely to seek prey of this type. This mirrors a similar situation in the wild, where invertebrates feature prominently in the diet of young cats because they tend to be easier to catch than other prey. Unfortunately, cats appear oblivious to the risk of chasing stinging insects such as bees.

The Scratching Post
Kittens And The Learning Process

Kittens are more likely to be injured, bitten or stung than older cats, largely because they do not appreciate the dangers that they can encounter outdoors. They also tend to explore their environment as part of the learning experience, investigating things that they have not seen before. Young cats usually learn quickly from bad experiences, and are less likely to repeat them in the future.

If your cat tries to swallow the insect and is stung at the back of the mouth or on the tongue, the throat may swell up dramatically, making it difficult for your cat to breathe. Take her to the vet as quickly as possible, trying to keep her airway open if necessary by pulling the tongue forward in the mouth, although your cat is unlikely to cooperate while you do this!

Younger cats allowed outside will often chase flying insects, such as butterflies and bees.

Super Sense

A cat has a much greater perception of the world around her than we do, relying less exclusively on her sense of vision and more on her other senses, particularly smell and hearing. This also enables her to gain a better insight into what has occurred recently in her patch and, especially, where she might find some tasty prey. By recognizing and respecting your cat's sensational wild side, you will deepen your understanding of her needs, allowing her to be herself at home.

The Feral Shadow

Today's domestic cats may appear far removed from their wild relatives, but beneath their home-loving exteriors their natural survival instincts remain essentially intact. The evidence for this can easily be found in most major cities, where colonies of feral cats—domestic cats that have reverted back to living in the wild—are likely to frequent urban areas such as railway embankments and docks and reside in empty or derelict buildings.

Effective hunting relies on excellent coordination and concentration as well as speed. Even so, most of the hunting attempts of domestic cats end in failure.

Feral kittens (below) can look often identical to their domestic counterparts, since they are usually descended from strays, but they will shun human contact.

Most feral cats occupy cities because there is more food to be scavenged, but they are highly adaptable and may reside in rural areas as well. Here they tend to live more solitary lives, relying more upon their hunting skills.

Night Creatures

Feral cats tend to be creatures of the night and are unlikely to be seen in the open until after dark, when they emerge from their hiding places to embark on their nocturnal lifestyles. These cats are usually the descendants of strays, which have been forced to eke out a living on the streets both by scavenging and hunting, just like their wild ancestors, seizing rodents and birds when the opportunity permits. The prolific

One characteristic of cats is that they are exceptionally patient hunters, with a feline being prepared to wait quietly for hours for a mouse to emerge into the open.

nature of cats means that these feral populations can grow quickly, creating colonies that can be bothersome for people in the neighborhood.

How Feral Cats Behave

Cats of this sort are not friendly; they avoid human contact, tending to skulk away in the shadows, with the eerie calls of the queens and aggressive encounters between toms creating what can easily become a fearful night-time cacophony. It is nearly impossible to tame an adult feral cat; as a result, cat welfare organizations do not attempt to do so when called in to deal with a colony. Instead, they try to trap the cats, arrange for them to be neutered then release them into the wild again. Ultimately, the colony to die out within a few years, since most feral cats have a much shorter lifespan than pampered domestic cats.

Even young feral kittens are usually much less responsive toward any human company than ordinary kittens. They will frequently hiss and scratch, rebuffing attempts to tame them, and are very likely to show a tendency to wander, often making it very difficult to domesticate them. They are also often unpredictable, and may lash out without any warning if they become anxious.

How Your Cat Works

Cats are able to
measure a jump with
great accuracy. The
muscular hind legs
power their progress,
and they touch down
first with outstretched
front legs.

Cats are natural athletes, able to run, climb, and jump easily. Domestic cats display all these skills, although in the case of their wildcat relatives, a greater degree of specialization can be seen, depending on their lifestyles.

Cheetahs, for example, rely exclusively on their pace, rather than climbing ability, to catch prey.

A Cat's Legs

The way in which cats run became clear as the result of a series of pioneering sequential photographs taken by Eadweard Muybridge. These were included in his book *Animal Locomotion*, which first appeared in print in 1887.

The photos revealed that the cat's gait actually changes as it increases its speed and begins running. Cats start by using a leg on one side of the body and then moving a leg on the opposite side of the body, continuing in sequence. For instance, they start with their right front foot, followed by the left hindleg, which gives increased

stability as their pace picks up. Once they are running, they use their hindlegs together, which are well muscled and provide the major propulsive thrust. Cats actually walk on their toes rather than their feet, the bones of which contribute to the length of the leg so they are able to cover more ground when running. This is further enhanced by a very flexible backbone that acts like a spring, helping them to increase their stride length even further. This ability is most evident in the cheetah (*Acinonyx jubatus*), which can cover around 10 percent more ground at each bound when running. As a result, it can close in on its prey that much more effectively.

A Cat's Claws

All cats have claws, although the cheetah's claws are not retractable, which helps this fast-moving feline maintain its balance even when

The claws of a domestic cat are normally kept hidden. They are sharp and pointed at the tips and curve slightly backward.

This sequence of images shows the way a cat moves, with its long stride allowing it to cover more ground at each bound.

turning at speed. Cats use their claws for a number of different purposes, perhaps the most obvious being to seize their prey. They also employ their claws when fighting and can inflict painful wounds with them. In a more passive role, cats use their claws for climbing and grooming. The claws themselves tend to wear down naturally, but in older pet cats that no longer spend much time outside, the claws may become overgrown quite easily and will need to be trimmed back. If your pet's claws are regularly getting caught in things, this is a likely sign that the claws are becoming rounded at their tips, which may also make walking difficult.

Coats As Camouflage

The patterns on the coats of wild cats, which look attractive and have led to their persecution for the fur trade, actually aid their hunting skills. The tiger's stripes, for example, help to break up its shape in the forests, providing what is sometimes known as disruptive camouflage.

The sandy color of lions helps them to merge in dry grassland, while leopards (*Panthera pardus*) in Africa usually display a typical spotted patterning on a light background, which helps to conceal their presence in open country. Leopards found in Asia, where these wildcats are more common in the forest, may appear black. They are sometimes described as black panthers, although they still retain the underlying leopard pattern and are exactly the same species.

The Importance Of Scent

Cats have a remarkable ability to detect scent from just a few molecules. They use their urine and droppings as scent markers, often depositing them in prominent positions within their territory. The penis of a male cat is located at the

A Cat's Tale
How Kittens Learn To Hunt From Their Mother

A cat's desire to hunt is partially instinctive, yet it also needs to be learned. It is a skill that is passed on from one generation to the next, with kittens learning by watching their mother. She instructs them once they are old enough to accompany her on hunting trips. They watch her stalk and catch prey, which she often brings back to them alive so they can learn how to kill their quarry. That is why kittens reared on farms rather than in kennels will prove to be the most effective mousers.

In contrast, most domestic cats kept as household pets have been reared in complete isolation from their natural prey. As a result, although they may instinctively catch a bird or a small mammal, they do not know how to kill it. They then end up pawing at the unfortunate creature in what is often mis-interpreted as a sign of sadistic cruelty rather than ignorance.

The Scratching Post
Why Does My Cat Scent Mark At Home?

Domestic cats will frequently mark their scent in the home, especially if another cat has recently been introduced. It is often wrongly assumed that a cat that suddenly refuses to use her litter box under these circumstances has suffered a breakdown in toilet training—but this behavior is really undertaken deliberately as a way of reinforcing her territorial claims.

Scratching of furniture may also occur for this same reason, with the claw marks and the associated scent from the sweat pads of the toes again serving as territorial markers.

rear of the body rather than on the underside, like a dog, so that when urinating against a tree or fence post, the urine leaves its scent at a height roughly in line with the cat's nose. This increases the likelihood that another cat passing the spot later on will easily detect the scent.

When a female is receptive for mating, the presence of chemical messengers, called pheromones, in her urine draws male cats from a wide area. This is attributed to the presence of the vomeronasal, or Jacobson's, organ, which is present in the roof of the mouth. Nerve impulses run from here to the part of the brain linked with reproductive behavior, and help to register the presence of a female nearby. When sniffing the air for this purpose, cats adopt a particular posture known as flehmening and breathe air into their mouths so the scent passes directly over this organ. The cat will lift his head, curling the lips upward and exposing the teeth in the upper jaw.

A Cat's Ears

Cats have far more acute hearing than we do, and this again directly aids their survival. Servals (*Felis serval*), for example, are able to pinpoint accurately the calls of rodents, which are made in the ultrasonic frequency range and are therefore inaudible to our ears. As a result, cats can obtain prey easily in grassland areas where rodents are hidden by vegetation. This is also a skill that helps domestic cats find rodents, while we ourselves may be unaware of their presence.

A Cat's Eyes

For hunting, cats tend to rely on a combination of sight and hearing rather than scent. Being active at night means that a cat's eyes have become adept at seeing images clearly in total darkness. This is possible because, while the basic anatomy does not differ from that of our own eyes, a cat's pupil narrows in bright light and becomes slit-like, restricting the light that enters the eye. In darkness the cat's pupil expands in diameter and becomes rounded in shape, allowing as much light as possible to pass through to the back of the eye, to the retina, where the image is formed.

In addition, there are two types of cells present on the retina, known as rods and cones. Cats have a higher percentage of rods, while we have

Anatomy Of A Cat's Senses

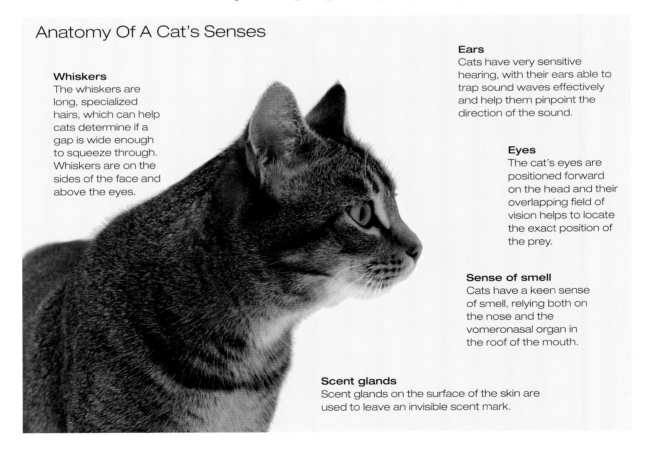

Whiskers
The whiskers are long, specialized hairs, which can help cats determine if a gap is wide enough to squeeze through. Whiskers are on the sides of the face and above the eyes.

Ears
Cats have very sensitive hearing, with their ears able to trap sound waves effectively and help them pinpoint the direction of the sound.

Eyes
The cat's eyes are positioned forward on the head and their overlapping field of vision helps to locate the exact position of the prey.

Sense of smell
Cats have a keen sense of smell, relying both on the nose and the vomeronasal organ in the roof of the mouth.

Scent glands
Scent glands on the surface of the skin are used to leave an invisible scent mark.

more cones. The result is that humans have better color vision than cats, but we cannot see so well in the dark because rods function more effectively when there is less available light.

Why Your Cat's Eyes Flash In The Dark

The other major structural difference in a cat's eyes is the presence of a reflective layer behind the retina, known as the *tapetum lucidum*. This acts like a mirror, reflecting the light back through the retinal cells and creating a clearer image. The effects of this layer are very obvious if you inadvertently shine a flashlight in your cat's face in the dark; the light will reflect back, highlighting her eyes and causing them to glow. The same thing happens, unfortunately, when a cat is crossing a road at night. In this case it is very likely to be blinded by the oncoming vehicle's headlights and may be unable to get out of harm's way. As a result, cats are more likely to be struck by a vehicle at night than during the daytime.

Binocular Vision

As a hunter, a cat needs to have acute senses and especially eyesight so it can determine exactly the right moment to pounce on its potential prey. Cats have binocular vision, which effectively gives them a three-dimensional image. As a result of their slight variance in position within the skull, each eye provides a slightly different but overlapping image.

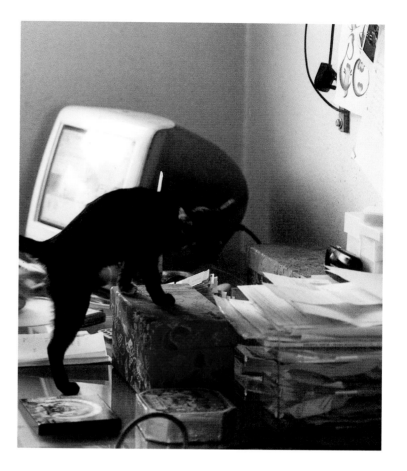

The brain can use the information to build up a very precise view of where the prey is located, enabling the cat to strike with pinpoint accuracy. Even a slight deviation off-target would otherwise enhance the likelihood of its quarry escaping.

The eyes in the cat's head are set pointing forward, which means that it has relatively poor peripheral vision, away from its immediate line of sight. Conversely, the cat's natural prey tend to have eyes located more toward the sides of the face, since this makes it

Cats are very adept at climbing around the home and often like to sleep near computers, which provide a source of warmth.

art of hunting is something that must be learned. In the wild, young cheetah cubs, in particular, may die from starvation after they have become independent, simply because they do not master this skill quickly enough.

A Cat's Tongue

Cats have a very muscular tongue, which serves a variety of purposes. Its most obvious feature is its rough surface, which enables the cat to rasp meat from the bone. It also serves to groom fur very effectively—just like a hairbrush—pulling out any loose hairs as it does so.

Unfortunately, the hairs are difficult for the cat to remove, so they may then be swallowed and can give rise to a hairball or fur ball in the stomach. Domestication increases the possibility of this problem in long-haired breeds, such as the Persian.

Kittens are not born with a full array of hunting skills. They lack effective binocular vision at first, which handicaps their hunting ability.

easier for them to detect movement nearby, which could indicate a stalking cat or other predator.

Learning Peripheral Vision

Not all cat breeds have a similar sense of peripheral vision. Siamese and their Oriental relatives are less adept in this respect than American shorthairs, for example. It is also a skill that cats need to learn, with young kittens not being able to use it for hunting until they are at least three months old. Even then, they will not prove to be such proficient hunters as their parents, confirming that the

Cats can use the tip of their tongue like a ladle to lap up water.

The tongue can also be expanded at its tip to act like a ladle. This then allows a cat to lap up water with relative ease, although cats usually do not drink significant amounts, because they meet most of their fluid requirement from that present in the tissues of their prey. Wild species such as the sand cat (*Felis margarita*), which is found in the semidesert areas of North Africa, the Middle East, and southwestern Asia, where water is in short supply, benefit most from this ability since it frees them from the need to drink regularly.

The Scratching Post
Why Are Cats Seen As Fertility Symbols?

The breeding cycle of the female cat is a result of the solitary lifestyle of her wild ancestors; it developed to ensure that conception occurs after chance encounter. Unlike most mammals, the act of mating triggers the release of eggs from the ovary so both the sperm and eggs are released into the reproductive tract at the same time. As a result, domestic cats have a reputation for being fecund simply because they conceive readily and continue to breed until the end of their lives. Females should be neutered at an early age to guard against unwanted kittens.

Cats are very adaptable in the way they can use their strength. While they have a potentially fatal array of teeth, female cats are able to carry their offspring in their mouths, without leaving a mark on them.

Bringing Home Prey:
What Your Cat Is Telling You

If your cat roams outdoors, she may sometimes return home with prey she has caught. Cats will often bring the unfortunate creatures back alive, depositing them in the home for you to find. A female cat normally displays this type of behavior when her litter reaches the weaning stage. It may very well be that the cat is displaying misplaced maternal instincts toward her immediate family, encouraging you to master the basics of hunting and killing prey! Trying to overcome this problem is not easy, but locking the cat flap at night and when you go out should help to ensure that you are not greeted by the local wildlife indoors when you return home.

Do not scold your pet for hunting her natural prey, because she will not understand what she has done wrong. Try to persuade your pet to transfer all her hunting instincts to her toys instead.

The Scratching Post
Bird-Chasing

Although it is distressing when cats catch birds in the backyard, they tend not to be very successful. That is why they can often be seen lying crouched down on the lawn, wagging their tail in what is often interpreted as a sign of frustration.

Domestic cats naturally prefer to prey on rodents, but small mammals such as mice are not numerous in the vicinity of most homes. Cats are therefore drawn to hunt birds, which present a much more difficult target, especially in a typical backyard setting where there is usually no natural cover to help the cat get close to its intended target. Therefore, the cat's strike rate under these circumstances is much lower than would normally be the case. Adult birds, in particular, are also alert and adept at remaining out of the grasp of domestic cats.

A Cat's Tale
Why Do Many Cats Have Tabby Coats?

Tabby patterning is common in non-pedigree cats because it can bring survival advantages. Kittens are less evident to predators because the patterning breaks up their outline. This ability to blend into the background may benefit the cat's hunting ability, making her less conspicuous to her prey—especially as cats tend to be creatures of the twilight zone.

Cats can not only jump horizontally, but are also able to use their hind legs like a spring to jump vertically as well. Servals use this ability to hunt birds, stalking close to a flock feeding on the ground, then jumping up and trying to knock one of them out of the air as they take flight.

How To Live With
Your Cat

When you understand your cat's breed, you'll understand her personality. All cats have a range of different temperaments, so there is a breed to suit your particular circumstances. Some breeds have been derived from naturally distinctive local cat populations, a chance mutation, or selectively bred by crossings with other breeds. More recently, domestic cats have been mated with small wildcats, too, to create new coat patterns and felines with attitude.

Personable Cats

Although they have a reputation for being rather independent, cats do appreciate companionship. A cat's breed affects the kind of companionship it prefers. Some breeds are sedate and will be happy as indoor cats; others are more active and need room to roam. If you have children, you need a breed that will accept and play happily with them.

The following types of cats are just a few examples of the variety of personalities that you can encounter. Please refer to the breed tables on pages 100, 113, 118, and 142 for a much more detailed breakdown of the characteristics of the different breeds.

The Affectionate Cat

Lively, entertaining, and affectionate cats with assertive natures, such as the Siamese, will be comfortable in a household where they will receive plenty of attention. Siamese, among the most vocal of cats, are not easily ignored. Teenagers especially will

A non-pedigree cat is a rewarding and self-reliant friend.

value the close bond they can establish with a Siamese. Short-haired cats like the Siamese require very little grooming.

The Tolerant Cat

If you want to be sure of a placid-natured cat, a safe choice is the ragdoll, a new breed noted for her tolerance. The ragdoll will enjoy being part of a family with young children, and she will be less likely to lash out if handled carelessly. This breed is named for the way her body becomes limp when relaxed. An amenable nature also means that she should not feel jealous of a new baby. She does require weekly grooming.

The Self-Reliant Cat

Your absence all day means that your cat deserves plenty of affection when you are home in the evening. Even so, since cats naturally tend to sleep during the daytime, they will adapt to this type of routine. Ordinary domestic cats will be content in this situation, because they are self-reliant and adaptable by nature.

The Companion Cat

The opportunity to have a single human companion will appeal to many cats: companionship will also

Long-haired Persians (left) enjoy human attention and the playful Russian blue (center) forms close emotional ties. Relaxed and friendly, the ragdoll (above) is the ideal family pet.

influence your choice. If you are living alone, there are a number of breeds that would suit you well. Short-haired and easy to groom, the Russian makes a reliable companion cat. If she comes to live with you as a kitten, the bond formed between you will be even stronger.

The Attention-Loving Cat

A home-loving cat that will not display any marked tendency to stray is likely to enjoy owners who have plenty of time to spend with them. Persian longhairs are ideal in this respect, and thrive on attention. They are bred in virtually every color variant recognized in the domestic cat, ranging from single solid color "selfs" to tabbies and calicos. Persian cats, however, do need daily grooming.

Are Pedigree Cats More Affectionate?

Studies of the differences in reactions between humans and non-pedigree, Persian, and Siamese cats have found that Siamese cats spend the most time interacting with humans, followed by Persians.

Both breeds of pedigree cat were found to be more dependent on their human owners than non-pedigree cats.

The stylish Siamese cat is affectionate and loyal.

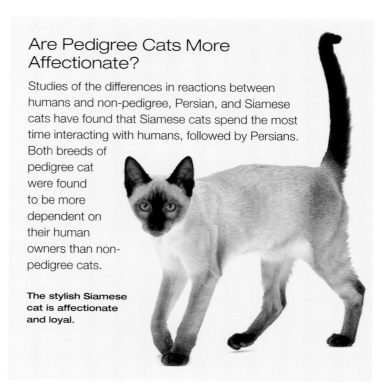

The Natural Breeds

Shorthairs And The Maine Coon
These breeds were initially developed by a process of natural selection from ordinary domestic cats, but later breed standards were set and certain attributes were specifically selected.

American, British, And European Shorthair
These breeds were descended initially from ordinary street cats, but were later crossed with Persians to improve their size.

British shorthairs are now bred in a wide range of color varieties, after crossings with Persians and Himalayans to introduce both oriental coloring and colorpoint patterning.

Maine coons (opposite) are a native North American breed.

Initially they had variable tabby markings often combined with white areas on their coat, but breeders strived to remove such patterning and create solid-colored or "self" varieties. They also attempted to standardize the white and colored areas of fur, aiming to create cats with the distinctive appearance of Dutch rabbits—colored areas on both the head and hindquarters separated by a white area on the center of the body and a white blaze extending down the front of the face. However, the breeders were not successful.

There are a number of different shorthair breeds, but all of them evolved in a similar way. The British shorthair is the best-known example of the group, but the others—with a more regional distribution—are the American and European shorthairs.

Maine Coon
A number of domestic cats arrived in the East Coast ports of the United States, carried in ships from all parts of Europe. These cats soon bred and increased in numbers around the ports, and it was here that the origins of the Maine coon lie. Unlike many subsequent breeds, it was shaped by its environment; a thick weather-resistant coat gave good protection against bitter winter weather and its large size meant it was a particularly

effective hunter. Maine coons fell out of favor when more exotic breeds were developed, but they started to become fashionable again in the 1950s due to a growing awareness among cat fanciers of the breed's heritage and the important role it played alongside the early settlers and homesteaders.

Maine coons still have a rather wild look—tabby and bicolor patterning is common, although there are "self" colors, too, such as black. They are friendly and self-reliant by

It is quite usual for Maine coons to have tufts of fur on the tips of their ears, which reinforce their wild appearance.

Domestic Breeds

Name	Origins	Personality	Ancestors	Page
American, British, and European shorthair	Europe, U.S.	Playful and resilient	Persian longhairs x street cats	98
Maine coon	Maine, U.S.	A natural explorer, friendly	European pure-bred x street cats	98
Cornish rex	Cornwall, U.K.	Athletic but happy house cat	A natural mutation	101
Devon rex	Devon, U.K.	Playful, a good mixer	A natural mutation	102
Selkirk rex	Wyoming, U.S.	Very affectionate	A natural mutation	103
Sphynx	Canada	Very affectionate	A natural mutation	104
Japanese bobtail	China	Very friendly	A natural mutation	105
Manx	Isle of Man, U.K.	Sociable, hardy	A natural mutation	105
Scottish fold	Scotland	Quiet and affectionate	A natural mutation	106
Scottish fold longhair	Scotland	Curious, good with children	A natural mutation	107
American curl	California, U.S.	Playful and placid	A natural mutation	108
Munchkin	Louisiana, U.S.	Brave and agile	A natural mutation	108

nature, but they definitely prefer to explore the outdoors rather than be kept permanently in the home. They are at home in cold climates where the natural profusion of their fur is displayed to best effect.

These are hardy, phlegmatic cats that enjoy a variety of situations and are playful by nature. Although they enjoy affection, they are not quite as strident as Siamese and will be very content in a family home. The range of colors and markings existing within these breeds represents virtually all those that have occurred within domestic cat bloodlines, and there are even color-pointed examples.

Unusual Breeds

Some of the most striking breeds of today are the result of individual mutations that have occurred—often at first among stray cats. Careful breeding programs have developed these changes in appearance. In rex varieties the mutation has affected the cat's coat so the normal fur structure is altered.

Cornish Rex

The oldest rex type is the Cornish rex, named after the county of Cornwall in the southwest of England, where in 1950 a strange-looking male kitten with a curly coat cropped up in a litter. His owner began breeding further examples, which she called rexes because of a similar mutation that she had noted in the rex breed of rabbits. In the Cornish rex, all the

The Scratching Post
How Many Layers In A Cat's Coat?

There are normally three layers of hair in a cat's coat. First are the outer guard hairs, which are relatively long, with the secondary guard hairs beneath them. The third layer of insulating down hairs, or awn, are shorter still and lie closest to the body.

hairs in the coat are shorter, with the secondary hairs reduced to the length of awn hairs (see box, above). Collectively, this creates the distinctive rippled or wavy appearance evident in the coat. To compensate for this lack of insulation, the body temperature of these cats is slightly higher. These rexes are very elegant and have a more wavy coat overall than their Devon relatives. They may look quite tall, especially because of their long, straight legs.

Lively and inquisitive by nature, the Cornish rex will settle well in the home. They are athletic cats and will climb readily and leap over relatively long distances. Rex cats are ideal if you do not want to spend long periods grooming your cat but would

The coloring of this attractive blue-cream and white Cornish rex is known both as dilute tortoiseshell and white and—particularly in North America—as dilute calico.

In spite of its relatively short fur, the Siamese patterning of this red-point Devon rex is clearly apparent.

prefer to play with her instead. To groom the Cornish rex you stroke smoothly from head to tail to keep the wavy coat in good condition.

Devon Rex

A second rex mutation occurred about 10 years later in the neighboring English county of Devon. The founder of the breed was a stray tomcat, which lived near a tin mine. He managed to elude any attempts to catch him. Nevertheless, he is believed to have mated with one of the local queens, who subsequently gave birth to a litter containing a rex kitten named Kirlee. The coat of the Devon rex is different from that of the

A Cat's Tale
Devon Rex: A Doglike Cat

Some owners have suggested that the Devon rex is more doglike in character than most cats, since it is very playful. It can even prove to be an adept retriever, bringing toys back to its owner, while retaining its natural feline agility, which means that a climbing frame for these cats would be appreciated.

Cornish rex, because it is made up largely of awn hairs with few guard hairs present. Its face has been compared to that of a pixie, partly due to its large, broad ears. Outcrosses to various other breeds have given rise to a wide range of colors, including the so-called Si-rex, which displays Siamese patterning. The most important feature in this breed is the quality of the coat, since Devon rexes can be prone to bald patches due to their naturally thin fur.

The Devon rex is a breed with real personality, possessing a highly playful nature. It will settle just as happily in a home with children and dogs as with an older person on their own, where it can be the center of attention. This rex again needs very little grooming, thanks to its thin coat, but is also more susceptible to the cold than other breeds. Its broad ears may need wiping occasionally, but never be tempted to poke anything down your pet's ear canal because this could be painful and harmful to delicate ears.

Selkirk Rex

The third well-known member of the rex group is much less likely to lose hair simply because it is a long-haired mutation. The Selkirk rex has a rather tousled appearance because of the curly nature of its coat; the curl extends even to its whiskers. Again, it cropped up as the result of an unexpected mutation—it was first seen in a female kitten that formed part of a litter given to an animal rescue shelter in Wyoming in 1987.

This rex breed was named after the nearby Selkirk Mountains, following the established tradition of naming these cats after their area of origin. It has again proved to be very different from other forms of rex, and not just in terms of appearance—in this case, the mutation is the result of a dominant gene. This means that mating a Selkirk rex with an ordinary cat should result in a high percentage of rex kittens in the resulting litter. The kittens themselves undergo an unusual change in appearance as they grow up;

they are born with a curly coat, which then becomes thinner and gains a wiry texture. The cat's long adult coat emerges just before it reaches one year old.

The Selkirk is a hardy and friendly addition to the list of rex breeds that are available today. Playful and with a relaxed attitude to life, it makes an excellent companion.

The Selkirk rex is the latest addition to the rex group of breeds. This is a blue-cream or dilute tortoiseshell example, with highly individual patterning.

The Scratching Post
Do Hairless Cats Occur In Different Colors?

Bicolor sphynxes are common, usually with a white area on the face extending onto the belly. It is possible to make out both the color and any patterning. This also applies to the Peterbald, a similar but rarer breed created by crossing a don hairless breed with Oriental-type cats in Russia in the early 1990s.

Sphynx

The most extreme member of this group of cats is the sphynx, also known as the hairless cat. Despite this description, it does have some fur, notably on the extremities of its body, as well as a very fine downy covering elsewhere. The mutation that gave rise to these highly unusual cats first occurred in Canada; some felines were then taken to Europe, where they became popular in France and the Netherlands.

The sphynx remains a rare breed even today, and needs special care. Its skin needs wiping regularly with a damp cloth or chamois leather to remove natural oily skin secretions, while its lack of fur means that it needs to be kept indoors. Otherwise, it will not only be at risk of becoming chilled in cold weather, but it's also very likely to suffer from sunburn and skin cancer in warmer climates. People who keep these cats find them very affectionate in spite of their odd appearance.

Two examples of a bicolor Sphynx. There is a distinctive difference in coloration between this black-and-white individual and the blue-and-white bicolor on the far right.

Tails And Ears

Other spontaneous mutations have affected the tails and ears of cats, and some of these have been developed to create distinctive breeds. Cats with shortened tails have been recorded from various localities over the course of centuries and this particular mutation is also clearly evident in the case of the bobcat. There are also a few spontaneous mutations that involve the ears, leading to cats with ears that are folded or curled, rather than standing erect.

Japanese Bobtail

The Japanese bobtail is recognized by its fairly rigid, curved stumpy tail, which measures between 2 and 4 in. (5 and 10 cm) long. It is covered with relatively long fur and resembles a pom-pom in appearance. The origins of this particular breed are believed to lie on the Asiatic mainland, almost certainly in China, from where these cats were brought to Japan over 1,000 years ago.

Although traditionally the short-haired form was more favored, Japanese bobtails with long hair have started to become prominent over recent years. However, the coat in this breed is not significantly longer than that of their shorthair counterparts.

The Japanese bobtail has gained a reputation for being a friendly and affectionate cat, possessing very distinctive call-notes.

Manx

The best-known tail mutation in the West is that of the Manx cat, which is named after the Isle of Man off England's northwest coast. Although Manx are often called tailless cats, there are actually three variants, all of which have a crucial role in the breeding process.

The completely tailless form is known as a rumpy, but two rumpies should not be paired together because of spine deformities associated with the tailless gene.

There are two other forms of the Manx: the stumpy, which has some evidence of a tail; and the longie, with a tail similar in length to that of an ordinary domestic non-pedigree. Manx are still rare cats today, partly because they tend to have small litters and only a percentage of the kittens

The Japanese bobtail is a stocky breed with a predominantly white coat, usually with a colored area on the top of the head. These cats tend either to be red and white as shown here, or red, black, and white—a tortoiseshell variant known in Japan as Mi-ke.

This classic tabby is a stumpy Manx, showing a discernible trace of a tail. The way in which the back curves up toward the rump is very clearly evident.

A Cat's Tale
Legend Of The Manx

The origins of the Manx are unknown, although there have been some romantic suggestions to explain the presence of these cats on the Isle of Man. One theory is that they may be descended from cats that swam ashore from wrecked galleons centuries ago, following the sea battle between British ships and the Spanish Armada in 1588. Alternatively, it is proposed that their ancestors may have been brought by even earlier seafarers visiting the island. These stories may have some truth in them, but what probably happened is that the mutation developed because cats on the island were isolated from those elsewhere on the mainland.

There was a well-known Manx in the United States called Nila-Blite Pola, who distinguished himself by winning a Best-in-Show award at the age of 13. There was also a Manx who regularly accompanied his bulldog companion to the South London Bulldog Show in Victorian times, with this seemingly odd couple attracting considerable attention at the time.

will be a true example of the breed, lacking any trace of a tail. Manx are bred in a range of colors and patterns corresponding to those associated with ordinary cats. In Canada a further development in their history occurred in the 1960s, when a long-haired version was established and became known as the Cymric, after the Celtic name for Wales.

Manx are well-adjusted, friendly cats, and this makes them an ideal choice for a household with children and dogs. Despite concerns about their health, they are surprisingly hardy and long-lived.

Scottish Fold

The Scottish fold was another natural mutation, which in 1961 arose in farm cats living near Coupar Angus, a village in Perthshire, Scotland.

These cats have folded ears and were originally called lop-ears because of a similar mutation known in rabbits. The folded ears can be passed directly from one generation to the next, because it is a dominant genetic trait. The change in ear shape has not impaired the cats' hearing in any way, but there is a potential problem associated with the mutation that may affect the legs and tail, which can become thickened, causing difficulty in walking. However, this problem is easily overcome simply by mating cats with folded ears to others with normal ears. Not surprisingly, given the wide variety of cats that have contributed to its bloodline,

Scottish folds now exist in a wide range of colors and patterns, although Siamese markings are not encouraged by the breed registry.

One reason for the popularity of these cats today is their friendly temperament, making them ideal companions around the home. They are quiet and affectionate, yet also instinctively curious.

Scottish Fold Longhair (Coupari)

The breeding program of the Scottish fold, originating from non-pedigree stock, meant that the long-haired gene was present in the bloodline

A Cat's Tale
Susie And Her Kittens

A shepherd named William Ross noticed that the ears of one of a litter of young cats were folded down at their tips rather than standing erect. Their owner offered him any other similar kitten born in the future, and although it was to be another two years before this promise could be fulfilled, this marked the beginning of the development of the Scottish fold breed. The timing was highly fortuitous because Susie, the original white cat who produced this kitten, was killed just three months later.

from the start. In the early days, long-haired felines were not favored in this breed, simply because the length of the fur tended to mask the distinctive, tight fold of the ears. It was not until the 1980s—some 20 years later—that the long-haired form began to attract any attention and was developed, again in the United States.

The breed was soon accepted for showing, although it has been known under a variety of names. These include Scottish fold longhair, Highland fold, and longhair fold, although ultimately this breed has become known as the Coupari in the United Kingdom.

Like the short-haired form, the Scottish fold longhair is quiet and affectionate and very friendly. It is also very curious but has an easygoing temperament which makes it good with children. It likes company, either human or another cat.

A black-and-white Scottish fold shorthair. Long-haired kittens can crop up in litters even when both parents are short-haired—they are recognizable by their fluffier appearance at this age.

Scottish folds are quite stocky cats, having been developed with outcrossings to British and American shorthairs. The one shown left is a red classic tabby.

A black long-haired American curl. The founder of this breed was long-haired, but short-haired felines are now also recognized for show purposes.

be up to six months before the curl has fully developed. The cat is able to move its ears, swiveling the tips so that they point toward each other, with the base of the ears quite firm. Tufts of hair are considered desirable at the tips of the ears.

At first, only long-haired forms of the American curl were recognized for show purposes, but subsequently, a short-haired form was developed. Since the breed developed from non-pedigree stock, there is a wide variety of colors available in this breed, including Siamese markings.

In terms of personality, these cats are very well adjusted. They are playful and yet also placid, making ideal companions, although care should be taken in homes with young children, who may be inclined to try to place their fingers or even objects into the cat's ear canal.

American Curl

America was home to another mutation affecting a cat's ears, which in some respects is the opposite of the Scottish fold. In 1981 a long-haired kitten with curled ears turned up on the steps of a cat-loving couple living in Lakewood, California, and later produced kittens with curled ears.

Interestingly, all newborn American curl kittens look as if they have normal ears. Only from the age of four to seven days do the ears start to change in those destined to be curls, with the tips turning back. Even then the change is gradual, and it may

Munchkin

The general conformity in the size of all breeds of cat helps to explain why the munchkin, named after the race of little people in *The Wizard of Oz*, proved to be such a controversial cat when it first appeared in 1983. It has greatly shortened legs, with its front legs measuring just 3 in. (7.5 cm) in length, compared with the more typical length of 7 in. (18 cm) in an ordinary cat.

The precise origins of the munchkin are largely unknown; the first was a stray called Blackberry, because of her black coat, found in the state of Louisiana. All of today's munchkins ultimately trace their ancestry back to her. While still controversial, and certainly not everyone's ideal cat, fears over the munchkin's state of health have proved unwarranted. This breed is popular in many parts of Europe as well as the United States, and exists in a wide range of colors. There is even a long-haired form.

Munchkins have more difficulty grooming themselves than other breeds since they are unable to scratch in the same way as other cats, and they are unable to run or jump as well as their long-legged relatives.

Yet in some respects, munchkins are more agile than other cats, capable of turning around and running under furniture more easily. They are lively and curious by nature and can run fast, scampering along like a ferret. Munchkins are also able to climb, but cannot jump well because of their shortened legs. Their small size does not inhibit them, though, because they are not even intimidated when living in the company of large dogs. They are friendly, confident, and intelligent cats, and make great companions for children.

A munchkin kitten at six weeks old. This short-legged breed comes in both longhair and shorthair forms.

Short Or Tall?

Domestic cats show very little variation in height, although larger breeds, such as the Norwegian forest cat, are taller than smaller breeds, such as the Siamese. On the other hand, there is nothing like the variation in size within cat breeds as exists in dog breeds. The reason for this is simple—the size of the African wildcat, which is the ancestor of all cats, varies relatively little through its range, whereas individual populations of the gray wolf (Canis lupus), which is the ancestor of all domestic dogs, can differ very markedly in size.

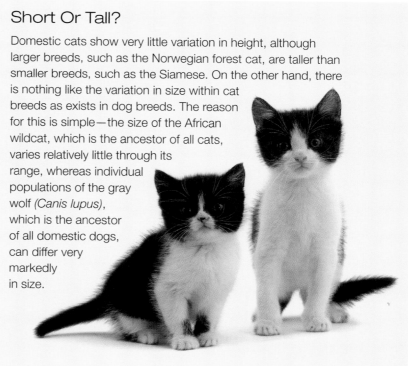

Beauty Breeds

The glowing green eyes of the chinchilla Persian (opposite) are very attractive. It takes some time for the eye color of cats to develop fully—all kittens initially have blue eyes.

The ragdoll (below) is a large breed that has been developed for its gentle, lovable temperament. This cat is a lilac bicolor.

The aim of breeding is to create new varieties and stable patterns. There are hundreds of different varieties that can be created within a number of breeds, especially when you consider not only color but also other characteristics, such as the range of tabby and tortoiseshell patterns.

In the case of some breeds, such as Orientals, breeders may not yet have created all of the possible variations. One of the trends of recent years among cat breeders has also been to create new breeds on the basis of their personalities rather than just their appearance.

Breeds Less Likely To Hunt

The hunting abilities of domestic cats can frequently prove to be a cause of distress to their owners, and over recent years, breeders have sought to curb these instincts by developing breeds that are more placid and less likely to display this type of behavior. In parts of Australia, the ownership of such cats is now being encouraged by the authorities, too.

Ragdoll

The origins of the ragdoll are shrouded in mystery; what is known is that the breed descended from a white long-haired cat at some time in the 1960s, which may have been either a Persian or Angora. She was hit by a vehicle while pregnant, and this gave rise to the strange belief that her offspring would therefore not be able to feel pain. Although this simply was not true, the claim attracted much media coverage at the time and helped to generate considerable interest in what was to become a distinct breed.

The pointed appearance of the ragdoll is believed to be from the introduction of birman stock into the bloodline, and there may have been some Burmese as well.

There are three recognized patterns associated with the breed: colorpoint ragdolls display the typical

The mitted feet of the ragamuffin are very similar to those of the ragdoll: both have white areas on their paws. They share a common ancestry, but the ragdoll is better known.

dark extremities on legs, feet, face, ears, and tail, offset against a lighter body color; bicolor ragdolls are similar but lack dark areas on their legs and feet; mitted ragdolls have dark legs with white feet resembling mittens.

All three breeds believed to have contributed to the ragdoll's ancestry are well-known for their relaxed natures, so it is not surprising that the ragdoll is very docile. It even gained its name because of its easy-going

The Scratching Post
What Is The "Flop" Factor?

The way in which ragdolls relax in their holder's arms has been dubbed their "flop factor" by the California breeder who developed the breed. The relaxed character of these cats extends outside the home as well, so they are generally not interested in hunting. As such, ragdolls have become an increasingly popular choice with owners who want a breed that will not prey on the local wildlife.

behavior when handled, usually making no attempt to struggle. This can make the ragdoll an ideal family pet, although younger children may manhandle such cats, taking advantage of their gentle, trusting nature.

Ragamuffin

There have been several other variants developed from ragdoll stock over recent years, of which the best known is the ragamuffin. This breed was developed in the mid-1990s, with the aim to retain the tolerance of the ragdoll but expand the available range of colors. While ragdolls had been restricted to the four traditional point colors—seal, chocolate, blue, and lilac—the ragamuffin introduced new colors, such as red points, and other variants as well, including tortie points, Persian, and Burmese colors.

This seal point ragdoll is the darkest color variety in this breed. Kittens are pale at birth, but they develop their points as they grow older.

Beauty Breeds: Western

Name	Origins	Personality	Ancestors	Page
Ragdoll	United States	Docile, gentle	Angora/Persian longhair x Birman	110
Ragamuffin	United States	Trusting, gentle	Ragdoll crosses	112
Persian	United Kingdom	Placid and very friendly	Turkish Angora	114
Spotted mist	Australia	Friendly and home-loving	Abyssinian x tabby Burmese	115

Different dark shading on the coat has given rise to a range of Persian varieties. The silver shaded shown here has much more extensive dark tipping on the individual hairs than a chinchilla, so the cat is darker in overall color.

Like the ragdoll, the ragamuffin is docile and relaxed and an ideal family cat. It is not a noisy cat, and can be quite self-contained.

Persian

The development of the Persian longhair marked the start of the selective breeding of cats. Such individuals were very prominent at the first cat shows in Britain in the late 1800s, and soon established a strong following in the United States. Persians have altered significantly in appearance since then; their coats have become even more profuse, while their faces are now broader and more rounded in shape. These cats have also been bred in an ever-increasing range of color varieties and patterns, with even Oriental colors, such as chocolate and lilac, transferred into the breed. Their brilliant colors have helped to ensure their continued popularity, although all Persians need a considerable amount of daily grooming to maintain their exquisite appearance.

The individual hairs can measure up to 5 in. (12.5 cm) long, with the coat being more profuse in winter than summer. This is believed to be a legacy of their Turkish Angora relative. The coat length does affect their markings, too, so that tabby patterning in particular is not as evident in Persians as in short-haired breeds.

However, this characteristic does enable the distinctive appearance of the smoke Persian to emerge very clearly, in a way that would be impossible with a sleek-coated cat. The effect is like watching smoke rising from a fire, as the name of this variety suggests, thanks to the way in which the coat parts as the cat moves, revealing its paler undercoat.

Spotted Mist

Australia is the only inhabited continent without an indigenous population of wildcats. Unfortunately, domestic cats have tended to fill this niche and proved to be a significant problem in some areas, where they have reverted to a feral lifestyle, preying on Australia's unique bird and animal life. During the late 1970s, Australian breeders created the spotted mist by means of a breeding program involving Burmese, ordinary tabby, and Abyssinian cats. The spotted mist has a strong following in its native country, although it still remains largely unknown elsewhere.

The spotted mist is a small, friendly cat, happy in the home and not tempted to wander into the bush.

Asian Cats

The Asian Group was created to encompass those breeds that resemble the traditional Burmese in appearance but differ in the markings. The actual temperament of the Oriental breeds, such as the Burmese and the Siamese, is different from that of Western breeds. Siamese in particular are very playful extroverts and are

Note the relatively triangular face of this seal point Siamese kitten, which is characteristic of the breed today. The so-called appleheaded form (see page 117)—the more traditional type that is now being recreated—has a rounder face.

relatively noisy by nature, too, calling loudly in their distinctive voices when they want their owner's attention.

Siamese

Early Siamese brought over from Asia to the United Kingdom in the late nineteenth century were frowned upon, not just for their appearance but also because of their delicate constitution. They were particularly susceptible to respiratory viruses, in an era before vaccination. Yet the Siamese ultimately became one of the most popular cat breeds in the world, perhaps peaking in numbers between the 1950s and 1980s.

Originally, Siamese had a body shape and size similar to an ordinary domestic cat, but selective breeding modified its characteristics to the distinctive triangular head profile and the lithe, athletic body associated with the breed today. Some breeders are now concentrating on reverting back to the traditional form, described as applehead Siamese. Outcrossing to other breeds means that Siamese are available in a wide range of colors.

Siamese, as well as Orientals, are highly active cats by nature and can be sexually precocious. In fact, these cats may breed successfully when just four months of age. They become especially demonstrative and call very loudly when in breeding condition, in contrast to the much more subdued behavior that is usually displayed by Himalayans and Persians.

Balinese

Breeders overlooked the occasional occurrence of long-haired kittens in early Siamese litters, but thanks to the efforts of cat fanciers in California and New York during the 1960s, these cats have now become established, along with their Oriental counterparts. It is thought that the gene responsible for their semi-longhair appearance—which is most clearly evident on the well-plumed tail—may have been introduced originally from Turkish Angora cats.

Long-haired Siamese may be known by different names depending partly on their coloration and on the cat registry, and this can sometimes lead to confusion. Traditional Siamese colors—seal, chocolate, blue, and lilac—may be deemed Balinese, with other color varieties called Javanese.

This Siamese (opposite) has the distinctive triangular head that is a characteristic of the modern breed.

Bred from Siamese stock, the Balinese (below) is similar in appearance but is easily recognizable by its plumelike tail, which reflects its longer coat. The lack of undercoat means that the coat appears relatively sleek despite its length.

Beauty Breeds

Name	Origins	Personality	Ancestors	Page
Siamese	Thailand	Active, extrovert	A natural mutation	117
Balinese	United States	Friendly, lively	Siamese x Turkish Angora	117
Burmese	Thailand	Playful, lively	Probably Siamese stock	119
Burmilla	United Kingdom	Loves company and attention	Burmese x chinchilla Persian longhair	119
Exotic	North America	Cute and cuddly	Persian longhair x American shorthair	120
Himalayan	United States	Relaxed and friendly	Siamese x Persian longhair	121
Havana and Foreign Lavender	United Kingdom	Lively and sociable	Siamese x black non-pedigree cat	121
Oriental shorthair	United Kingdom	Lively and playful	Siamese x non-pedigree cat	122
Korat	Thailand	Alert and playful	Unknown	123
Birman	Burma	Affectionate and quiet but outgoing	Unknown	124
Angora	United Kingdom	Extrovert but affectionate	Oriental shorthair crosses	127
Turkish Angora	Turkey	Aloof but can be affectionate	Unknown	127
Russian	Archangel, Northern Russia	Quiet but friendly	Unknown	128
Siberian	Siberia	Adventurous, but in danger of traffic in towns	Longhair street cats	128
Norwegian forest cat	Scandinavia	Fond of exploring, but in danger of traffic in towns	A natural mutation	129
Egyptian mau	Europe	Intelligent, reserved	Egyptian street cat paired with non-pedigree tom	131
Abyssinian	Ethiopia	Friendly, adaptable	Ethiopian street cat x British cats	132
Somali	United Kingdom	Good with children and pets	Abyssinian x Turkish Angora	132

Friendly and lively, Balinese are bred in a wide range of colors, but their points may not appear as dark as those of Siamese. The fur of these cats has an attractive, fine, silky texture. The lack of a thick undercoat helps to prevent the coat from developing mats, although daily grooming will still be essential.

Burmese

The contrast between the points and the body color of these cats is less marked than in their Siamese close relatives. The traditional color associated with the Burmese is sable, which is dark brown, with the mask and ears being a slightly darker shade than the body, and the underparts paler. Other coat colors may be known as Malayan.

These cats have been developed on slightly different lines in North America and Europe, so there is a noticeable variation in appearance between the two types. In fact, at North American shows there are often separate classes for European Burmese, which are recognizable by a less stocky appearance than their American relatives.

Playful and lively by nature, Burmese make excellent companions.

Burmilla

Show cats are judged by their overall appearance, as well as by markings, colors, and similar features. Judging standards generally do not focus on the cat's temperament, although show

Not all cat associations recognize this cat (top left) as a red Burmese. Some regard it as a red Malayan, which can create confusion.

The traditional form of the Burmese is known as the sable in North America, but is better known simply as the brown in the United Kingdom and elsewhere. Such cats are seal brown in color, slightly paler on the underside of the body, as shown here.

The burmilla is a very striking breed—its exact appearance depends on the extent of dark pigmentation on the tips of individual hairs.

Exotic kittens (below right) have inherited their flat faces from their Persian ancestor. This breed has become very popular over recent years.

cats need to be tractable so they can be assessed; aggressive felines are likely to be disqualified. Nevertheless, it was quite revolutionary when the burmilla breed came into being in the early 1980s in the United Kingdom. For the first time the temperament of this friendly breed (and other members of the emerging Asian Group) was incorporated into its show standard.

The burmilla arose by chance after an accidental pairing between a Burmese and a chinchilla Persian. The result is a stunning short-haired breed, displaying either darker tipping or shading on its coat, with tabby markings on its legs.

Not only is the burmilla beautiful; it also makes an excellent companion, being attentive and very responsive by nature, thriving on company.

Exotic

Although the look of the Persian longhair appeals, you may not want the responsibility of having to comb and groom its coat consistently every day. This was exactly the thinking that led to the development of the exotic, which has now become one of the most popular breeds in North America. It was created by crossing Persians and American shorthairs, while in Europe, British or European shorthairs were used in a similar way, also paired with Persians.

Cute and cuddly, the exotic is available in a range of colors. It is a friendly, home-loving cat that has been compared to a teddy bear, thanks to its plush, easy-care coat.

Himalayan (Colorpoint Longhair)

This large breed was created as the result of an experiment in feline genetics during the 1920s. It represents the fusion of the pointed characteristic of the Siamese with the type and coat length of the Persian longhair. The so-called Himalayan gene causes the body extremities to develop darker fur, in contrast to the fur on the body itself, and explains the breed's name—although in the United Kingdom these cats are better known as colorpoint longhairs. Just as the number of Siamese varieties has grown significantly over recent years, there is now a much wider range of color varieties in this breed.

In terms of their temperament and general behavior, Himalayans resemble Persians much more closely than Siamese.

Havana And Foreign Lavender

A breeding program has also been used to re-create the green-eyed strain of Siamese, which became extinct in the 1920s. In the 1950s, a chocolate-point Siamese mated with an ordinary black non-pedigree, giving rise to green-eyed chocolate kittens with a decidedly Siamese appearance. They were originally called foreign browns, and later became known as Havanas. At this same time, the foreign lavender, was also introduced, with the term "foreign" simply indicating that the appearance of these cats did not correspond to the round-faced, cobby appearance of British shorthairs. They now tend to be known as lavenders, with the description of "foreign" having mostly fallen out of favor.

These two breeds were among the

The relatively long and slender body—which is characteristic of the Oriental breeds—is very evident in the Havana.

The lavender (below left) and the Havana (below right) are two original varieties from what is now known as the Oriental Group. The lavender is better-known as the lilac in the United Kingdom.

Orientals have a body shape that clearly corresponds to that of the Siamese, but they are not colorpointed. The depth of coloration can vary slightly between individuals, as seen in these two examples of an Oriental lavender—or lilac, as this color is known in the United Kingdom.

earliest examples of the rapidly expanding group now known as Oriental shorthairs, which tend to share a similar temperament.

Oriental Shorthairs

What sets Oriental shorthairs apart from Siamese is that they are bred in solid colors with many other combinations—such as bicolors, tabbies, and torties. The group is so extensive in terms of the possible varieties that it offers tremendous potential for breeders interested in feline genetics. There have been attempts to create an Oriental longhair category—corresponding to the Balinese, which is the longer-coated form of the Siamese—but these cats have not become very popular. The description Oriental is now used for all the cats in this group, while the term Siamese serves to identify only those with pointed patterning.

Since they have descended mainly from Siamese stock, Orientals have a very similar temperament; they are lively and demonstrative and demand attention from their owners on occasion. Orientals have identical requirements to Siamese. Their sleek coats need little grooming, thanks to their relative lack of undercoat, and they are likely to prove sexually precocious, with queens maturing early—sometimes when just four months old. Early neutering to prevent unwanted kittens is advisable.

A pair of young Korat kittens playing together. Although such games may appear quite rough, they very rarely result in injury.

Korat

There has been a long tradition of keeping cats in Thailand, often in association with the monasteries. The Siamese originated here—its name is based on Siam, the old name for Thailand. The Korat is named after its home province in the northeast of the country, where its ancestors may have lived for over 750 years.

A Cat's Tale
Why Are Korats Quite New To The West?

There was once a fairly widespread tradition in Asia that some breeds of cat or dog could not be bought—they could only be given as gifts to outsiders to mark a particular honor. The first Korat recorded outside its homeland was a single cat brought to London in 1896. The breed then remained totally unknown in the West until 1959, when a pair was given to the American ambassador to Thailand.

The traditional color of these cats is blue, with the coat itself having pale tipped hairs that give a silvery sheen, although lilac examples are now seen occasionally, as are chocolate. The Korat's fur, in common with the Siamese, is very short and fine in texture as well as sleek, outlining the body shape of these cats. Korats have a very distinctive heart-shaped head with large, stunning green eyes that possess a decidedly luminous quality.

Alert and playful by nature, this home-loving breed was traditionally given as a wedding gift to young couples in its native province, since it was believed to bring prosperity. If you are searching for an exotic breed with a long history, and a quiet, friendly nature, then you may want to consider the Korat. With a short, fine coat, its grooming needs are very modest, and regular stroking of the fur will contribute to the coat's gloss.

Birman

Although most breeds from southern Asia are short-haired, there is a long-haired pointed breed from this part of the world that is now widely recognized as the birman. It is believed that the ancestors of this breed were temple cats from Burma, although similar cats are known in Tibet. A pair was given in 1919 as a gift to two Western explorers who had helped the monks repel an attack on their temple. The tom died on the long journey back to France, but the female gave birth to a single kitten and thus founded the birman breed outside its homeland. A number of other breeds subsequently contributed to its development.

The birman's markings are unique, with white areas known as gloves on the front paws and more extensive white areas called laces extending up to the hocks on the hind legs. Birmans exist in a wide range of color varieties, although some breed registries only accept the traditional point colors of seal, blue, chocolate, and lilac. The eyes are the vivid blue associated with cats of this type.

Quiet yet outgoing by nature, the birman has proved to be an affectionate and tolerant breed by nature. Few other breeds develop such a strong bond with their owners.

The Korat has an unusual facial shape, which sets it apart from other cats of Oriental origin. It is purebred, with a history dating back many centuries.

The birman is a composite breed, developed from just two felines brought to France. The Himalayan was one of the main breeds used in its later development.

The Changing Face Of Popular Breeds

The Turkish Angora is believed to be the original ancestor of the Persian longhair, in spite of the fact that they no longer resemble each other. By selectively breeding over time for particular features such as coat length, it is possible to create a breed with a completely different appearance. Persians have actually changed dramatically over the past 100 years or so. The earliest photographs of prize-winning Persians highlight felines with coats that were much shorter overall than those seen today. Their faces were also significantly different, too, at that stage—relatively narrow and elongated, rather than broad and flat.

In contrast, the facial shape of the Siamese has become modified in a completely different way, again as the result of selective breeding. The very distinctive triangular-shaped face associated with the contemporary breed is unlike that of the first Siamese seen in the West, which had much more rounded faces and larger, less slanted eyes.

Some breeders are now working to reestablish the original appearance of the Siamese, describing their cats as apple-head or old-style Siamese, to avoid confusion with those more commonly seen today.

Angora And Turkish Angora

Farther to the west in Asia, Turkey was home to the Angora breed for many centuries, which in turn is believed to be the ancestor of the Persian longhair. These cats were originally named after the ancient capital city of Angora. They are traditionally white with blue or orange eyes, but there is also an odd-eyed form, called Ankara kedi, which has one blue eye and one orange.

Unfortunately, the breed had become very scarce by the beginning of the twentieth century, so the Turkish government mounted a conservation breeding program at the Ankara zoo in the 1960s. Some of these cats were later sent to breeders elsewhere around the world.

Meanwhile, other breeders had set out to re-create the Angora using Oriental shorthair crosses. The confusion created by these two different strains of the Angora led to the original Angora being described as Turkish Angora, while the re-created breed was simply called the Angora to distinguish between them. Although similar in appearance, the separate bloodlines are not mated together and some breed registries do not recognize both strains.

The Angora has a slightly longer head and bigger ears than the traditional form. In both cases, the fur is soft and silky with no dense undercoat. The Angora matures earlier and has larger litters than the Turkish Angora, as well as tending to be much more vocal.

Perhaps unsurprisingly, in view of its ancestry, the Angora also more closely resembles the Siamese in terms of its temperament. Turkish Angoras, in contrast, are not generally as extrovert as the modern Angora, having a more aloof nature. They will nevertheless prove to be highly affectionate and loyal companions.

The Turkish Angora (opposite and below) is believed to be the forebear of today's Persians; some early photographs reveal a very close similarity in appearance. However, since then the coat of the Persian has become much more profuse and its facial shape has been altered by selective breeding.

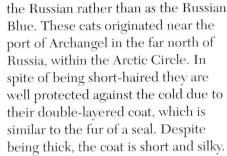

the Russian rather than as the Russian Blue. These cats originated near the port of Archangel in the far north of Russia, within the Arctic Circle. In spite of being short-haired they are well protected against the cold due to their double-layered coat, which is similar to the fur of a seal. Despite being thick, the coat is short and silky.

Friendly by nature toward people whom they know well, Russians can prove rather aloof toward strangers. They are quiet cats by nature.

The Siberian (above) has evolved over centuries with very little deliberate human interference.

The blue form of the Russian (below right) is the traditional color variety. The vivid emerald green eye color is a characteristic feature of the breed.

Russian

From much farther north in Asia comes the Russian. This very distinctive breed is traditionally blue in color, although over recent years both black and white felines have emerged so it is now known simply as

Siberian

Another native Russian breed that has become much more widely known outside its native land since the 1990s is the Siberian. It was also called the Siberian forest cat for a period because of its similarity in appearance to another northern breed, the Norwegian forest cat.

The Siberian arose in a very inhospitable climate and its appearance has been shaped largely by natural forces rather than by selective breeding. There is always a danger that these distinctive features will be lost once such cats become more widely kept for show purposes. Siberians normally display tabby markings on their coat and tend to be bicolor, reflecting their non-pedigree origins. They have a glossy, water-repellent topcoat with a very thick undercoat beneath, which provides good insulation in the cold.

Although friendly by nature, the Siberian retains an independent

streak to its character, often displaying a tendency to roam in a similar way to its ancestors, even when the weather is bad outdoors. As a result, they are not suited to an urban environment, where they will be at risk from traffic. The Siberian is not a good choice as a pet that will be kept permanently restricted indoors.

Norwegian Forest Cat

Another very hardy breed, the Norwegian forest cat is well protected against the elements, thanks to its double-layered coat. The woolly undercoat provides good insulation against the cold, while the glossy topcoat serves to prevent the cat from becoming chilled by rain and snow. These cats have been kept in their Scandinavian homeland for centuries, but their exact origins are obscure.

Active by nature, Norwegian forest cats are ideally suited to being kept in a more rural environment rather than being confined to an urban one. Their fondness for going exploring means they may be at greater risk of getting hit by cars. Their coats are usually dark colors combined with white and tabby markings. They have a friendly temperament and enjoy a busy household with lots of children.

Well-equipped to thrive outdoors in the cold climate of its homeland, the Norwegian forest cat likes to roam. It is therefore not a good choice if you are looking for a cat to live indoors permanently.

Egyptian And African Cats

Surprisingly, breeds from Egypt and the adjacent area of Africa are rare, although it is said that the Egyptian mau may have an ancestry that extends back to the early days of the cat's domestication. Cat breeds of African origins are essentially unknown, with the exception of the Sokoke and the Abyssinian.

Egyptian Mau

The Egyptian mau is similar in appearance to cats represented in Ancient Egyptian tombs. The founder of the breed was a street cat taken from Cairo to Italy, where she mated with a non-pedigree tom in the early 1950s. The spotted tabby breed was later developed in the United States, where it remains scarce even today.

The spots on the Egyptian mau's coat are mostly randomly distributed, although they may run in stripes down the spine. The spots vary in size and shape, but are quite distinct against a paler background.

A well-balanced temperament is a characteristic feature of the Egyptian mau, reflecting its basic non-pedigree roots. This breed has an adaptable and affectionate nature, but is not likely to prove extroverted by nature, as is the Siamese for example. Its innate intelligence means that it learns quickly, and it will soon adapt to new surroundings as a result.

The Scratching Post
Are All Blue-Eyed Cats Deaf?

Most blue-eyed white cats are likely to be less responsive than other varieties, simply because they suffer from a congenital deafness. Odd-eyed whites are likely to be afflicted by deafness on the side of the face corresponding to their blue eye.

It has also been suggested that blue-eyed white queens, in particular, may be rather nervous by nature, but this may simply be related to their disability.

The white cat seen right is an odd-eyed female, with a part-Bengal ancestry.

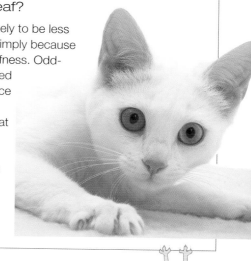

The roots of the Egyptian mau (left and opposite) lie in Egypt, but essentially it is a tabby that has been styled to resemble representations of early domestic cats, rather than being a breed of true antiquity.

Abyssinian And Somali

Although the Abyssinian was originally an African breed, virtually all of its development occurred in Europe. A single feline was supposed to have been brought back from Abyssinia—now known as Ethiopia—by a soldier in 1868 and is said to have shaped the breed. The range of colors that exist in this breed has expanded significantly over recent years, with the original color described as "usual" in the United Kingdom, but better known as ruddy in North America. The coat of the Abyssinian consists entirely of hairs with alternating light and dark bands, which is known as ticked tabby patterning. They have a dark tip to the tail, but selective breeding has removed the rings and bars on the legs, which are a feature of most tabbies. Abyssinians retain the characteristic M-shaped marking on the forehead, while the presence of ear tufts transforms these cats into a semblance of miniature wildcats.

Careful selective breeding has shaped the Abyssinian breed. Its subtle patterning is known as ticked tabby.

A Cat's Tale
The Somali
Name

The longhair form of the Abyssinian is known as the Somali; the name was chosen because this country lies next to the former Abyssinia.

The Somali was considered undesirable by breed registries until the 1970s.

The Somali—the long-haired form of the Abyssinian—has no direct links to Africa; it was developed in the West. How the long-haired gene entered the Abyssinian bloodline is not clear, but it may be the result of early crossings with Turkish Angoras. Somali kittens tend to be slightly darker in color than adult cats, such as this chocolate example.

The long-haired version of the breed, called the Somali, is similar in all respects to the Abyssinian, apart from its coat length, although this is not as profuse or long as in many other long-haired breeds.

Abyssinians and Somalis are full of character, and very friendly and affectionate. They also tend to have an adaptable nature, and are content to live in a home alongside children and other pets, including dogs.

Wild Styles

Many of these cats are rare, but are becoming increasingly popular breeds. Their personalities are influenced by their wildcat ancestry.

Early Wildcat Breeds

Cat fanciers in the first half of the twentieth century concentrated on developing breeds without any reference to wildcats, but from the late 1950s onward breeders began to reassess the appearance of domestic cats alongside that of their wild relatives. Some embarked on breeding programs to create miniature versions of larger wildcats.

Bombay

The Bombay, which resembles a black panther, was initially created in the United States, thanks to the efforts of a Kentucky breeder named Nikki Horner. She chose a Burmese to create the desired appearance or "type," and a black American shorthair to give the desired coloring. The fur of the Bombay is short and sleek with a distinctive sheen. The eyes of adult cats are a bright shade of gold or copper, although, as with all kittens, these are blue in color at first and subsequently change to gray before assuming their distinctive coloration.

A similar breeding program was carried out in Britain, but the British Bombay differs slightly in appearance from its North American relative; the British form of the Burmese has a lighter build, and British rather than American shorthairs were used in the breeding program.

Since it is bred from existing domestic cat bloodlines, the Bombay's temperament is very similar to that of its Burmese ancestor, but slightly more placid, given the American shorthair input into its ancestry.

Ironically, Scottish wildcats (opposite) are now an endangered species, partly because matings with domestic cats are common, creating hybrid kittens.

The Bombay (below) is defined by its black color as much as its type. This reflects the original inspiration behind its development.

Spotted patterning has become very popular in recent years. The ocicat is one breed that has been developed with patterning of this type.

The ocicat has spots roughly the size of thumbprints in a spotted tabby pattern over the body. The distinctive lines at the corner of the eyes are known as "mascara lines."

Ocicat

Other breeding programs have led to the development of domestic cats that display wildcat markings on their coats. The first breed of this type was the ocicat, although this was not created deliberately—it came about in 1964 as the result of an attempt to breed a Siamese with Abyssinian patterning. Its breeder, Virginia Daly of Michigan, neutered the first kitten that displayed this patterning, but then decided that she liked its pretty spotted appearance so much that she repeated the original mating. Several spotted kittens were then born; their patterning is similar to that of the American wildcat called the ocelot

(*Felis pardalis*). Originally, these cats were known under two names— ocellete, meaning "small ocelot," and accicat, because of the fortuitous nature in which the breed came into existence; these were then combined to create the name ocicat. Once again, a separate strain of ocicat was created in Europe, but not until 1984.

Combining the Siamese and Abyssinian together in this way has resulted in a highly affectionate breed that interacts wonderfully with people, but hates to be left alone in the house. They can be trained to play fetch or walk on a leash, and are wonderful with children.

California Spangled

After being horrified by the level of poaching of leopards (*Panthera pardus*) in Africa in 1971, Hollywood scriptwriter Paul Casey bred the California spangled in the image of a wildcat to raise awareness of the plight of all wildcats around the world.

Working over 11 generations to reach his goal, he used purebred, non-pedigree, and even feral cats for his ambitious program. He traveled more than four continents to locate the cats he needed, including Siamese, British shorthair, Manx, and a street cat from Cairo, among others. To guarantee maximum publicity for his campaign, the first California spangled kittens were offered for sale in an exclusive mail-order catalog in 1986.

The California spangled's obvious spotted patterning and dark tail tip really do mirror that of a wildcat, especially when it is seen in profile with its long body and low-slung back. Paul Casey's campaign struck a chord with cat owners, and soon there was a waiting list for these cats in spite of their high price tag.

Although it may look like a wildcat, the California spangled has proven to be an excellent companion breed, affectionate but not demanding of attention. Its easygoing nature reflects its varied ancestry. However, these are athletic, active cats, as suggested by their muscular appearance, so they will not be happy if kept indoors.

A Cat's Tale
Are They Friendly?

Relying on domestic cats to create new breeds that resemble wildcats is a simpler process than using real wildcats, and the kittens have a better temperament. The introduction of wildcat genes initially creates offspring that do not enjoy close contact with people—and will actively try to avoid humans, even if the cats are reared in domestic surroundings rather than in a kennel.

The California spangled remains a rare and exclusive breed, even today. Kittens display their characteristic patterning at birth.

Later Breeds

The use of wildcats themselves to introduce attractive new patterning into domestic cat bloodlines is controversial. Already this type of breeding program has created the Bengal, which now ranks as one of the most popular breeds in the world today. The resulting breeds of this type also tend to be larger in size than typical domestic cats, because of their wildcat ancestry.

Bengal

As breeds with the appearance and markings of wildcats were being developed, there were people thinking about the possibilities of deliberate hybridization to achieve a similar goal. In 1963 a geneticist named Jean Sugden mated an Asian leopard cat (*Felis bengalensis*) with an ordinary black domestic cat to see if it was possible to transfer the striking markings of the Asian leopard cat into the domestic cat bloodline. Crossings of this type are difficult to achieve, even under carefully controlled conditions, because of both fertility problems and a lack of compatibility between the cats themselves.

In this case, a single kitten named Kinkin resulted, but in due course, when paired back to the Asian leopard cat, both spotted and plain-coated kittens were born in another litter. Later Sugden also introduced stray tomcats into her breeding program, but other breeders attracted by this concept subsequently used a variety of purebred cats, including the Abyssinian and the Egyptian mau. Siamese blood was introduced to the Bengal bloodline early in its development, and this has resulted in the creation of the stunning snow-marbled variety, which has marbled patterning on a whitish background and blue eyes.

The Bengal now ranks as one of the most popular of all breeds

The Bengal started something of a tradition in the naming of wildcat hybrid breeds—its name is derived from the scientific name of its wildcat ancestor. This practice continued with the chausie (see page 140).

worldwide, and is available in an increasing number of color varieties.

Early Bengals were much shyer and less temperamentally stable than a typical domestic cat, but are now as friendly as any other domestic cat although likely to be reserved with strangers. Like their Asian ancestor, they often display a fondness for water—even jumping into a bath or having a shower. Bengals are large cats and tend to be active by nature compared with other domestic breeds; they especially enjoy games where they can leap onto make-believe prey. A climbing frame for

Bengals still possess sharp hunting instincts and have very powerful feet, but they are now just as friendly as more traditional breeds.

them will be well used, since their wild ancestors sometimes hunt in the trees. Bengals often sound different from other cats, vocalizing just like Asian leopard cats.

Chausie

The stunning appearance of the Bengal has subsequently led to a number of other attempts to transfer wildcat markings into domestic strains, creating further new breeds. One is the chausie, a result of hybridization with the jungle cat

(*Felis chaus*), which has a naturally golden or sometimes pure black (melanistic) coloration rather than spots. First attempts at crossbreeding began in the late 1960s but chausies only really became prominent in the 1990s, and they still remain better known in North America than elsewhere. They are only bred in three varieties corresponding to that of their jungle cat ancestor: a brown ticked tabby and two black varieties, one of which has silver tipping to its fur, making its coat sparkle when it moves. Ideally, chausies also have distinctive tufts of fur sticking up on the tips of their ears.

As befits their wild ancestry, chausies are highly active cats, but are generally smaller than the jungle cat. Male chausies weigh 20 pounds (9 kg) on average, tending to be larger than females—a typical characteristic seen naturally in most wildcats, and larger breeds of domestic cat, too.

Savannah

Perhaps the most revolutionary breeding program of this type involved another African wildcat, the serval (*Felis serval*). The serval is much larger than the ordinary domestic cat, weighing about 40 pounds (18 kg), and has a spotted coat, long legs, a slender body, and bat-like ears, which foster extremely acute hearing.

The first attempts to create a breed by mating servals with domestic cats began in the mid-1980s by a Pennsylvanian Bengal cat enthusiast named Judy Frank. Domestic breeds that contributed to its subsequent development include Oriental shorthairs, the Egyptian mau, and the Bengal. Named after the grasslands of Africa where the serval is relatively common, savannahs are rare even in the United States.

Savannahs have proved to be agile and playful cats and their distinctive appearance is eye-catching, with their spotted patterning extending over their bellies, and striped legs. Just like their wild ancestor, they also have relatively large ears, long legs, and powerful paws, but in other respects they do not differ significantly from other breeds. Regular cat food suits them well, and they can be litter-trained without difficulty.

A Cat's Tale
The Two Types Of Wildcat, African And European

There are two forms of wildcat, which are regarded as separate species. The European wildcat (*Felis silvestris*) is found both in Europe and western parts of Asia. It is a particularly shy and secretive species. Its African cousin (*Felis lybica*) is typified by a sandier coat coloration and a bolder nature. Not surprisingly, today's domestic cats were originally bred from the African wildcat, but once they were brought into Europe, matings with the European wildcat probably occurred.

Natural Cross: Wildcat and Domestic

The free-ranging nature of cats, especially feral felines, means that they are likely to come into contact with their wild relatives. However, there are no confirmed cases of breeds that have developed from such matings. The low success of this crossbreeding may be due to the small litters born as a result. In addition, young cats in the wild, just like other creatures, often do not survive to maturity and male offspring are likely to be infertile.

Pixiebob

The pixiebob, a rare American breed, was thought to be the result of mating between a domestic cat and a bobcat (*Lynx rufus*). A successful mating of this type seems highly unlikely, given

"Wild" Domestic Breeds

Name	Origins	Personality	Ancestors	Page
Bombay	United States	Placid	Burmese x black American shorthair	134
Ocicat	U.S.; later bred in Europe	Affectionate people cat	Siamese x part-Abyssinian	136
California Spangled	United States	Athletic and easy-going	Many, such as Cairo streetcat, Manx, Siamese, British shorthair	137
Bengal	United States	Reserved but friendly	Asian leopard cat x black domestic cat; later, Egyptian mau, Abyssinian	138
Chausie	United States	Lively and athletic	Jungle cat x domestic cat	140
Savannah	United States	Agile and playful	Serval x domestic cat; later, Bengal and Egyptian mau	141
Pixiebob	United States	Curious and playful; likes to nest	Natural mutation of the domestic cat	142
Singapura	Singapore	Placid, happy in groups	Street cats	143
Wild Abyssinian	Singapore	Bonds easily, independent	Street cats	144
Ceylonese	Sri Lanka	Bonds easily; independent	Street cats	144
Sokoke forest cat	Kenya	Affectionate and active	Street cats	145

characteristics within these groups. Although initially such cats tend to behave and display the instincts of wildcats, it can be possible, over several successive generations, to domesticate them again, especially by outcrossing to domestic breeds.

Singapura

The diminutive Singapura was the first breed of this wild-domesticated type to be recognized over the past century. Its ancestral origins are thought to lie in the harbor area of the Asian city of Singapore, on the northeast of the island, where the cat was discovered in 1974 by an American couple, Hal and Tommy

the wide variance in size between the cats concerned and the fact that the bobcat belongs to a completely separate group. Nevertheless, there is no denying the fact that the pixiebob does resemble a bobcat, with its spotted coat and shortened tail. On the other hand, these features are also sometimes seen in domestic cats.

The pixiebob has a reputation for its great sense of curiosity, readily exploring its environment, and having favorite retreats around the home. It is also very playful.

The Cat Pack

In various parts of Asia and Africa there are cat populations that have grown up in relative isolation, and interbreeding has led to the development of individual

The pixiebob (above) may look wild but is a friendly breed. These cats sometimes have extra toes on their feet.

The Singapura is the smallest breed of cat in the world, weighing under 6 lb. (2.7 kg).

Tabby patterning in its various forms is a feature that unites the wild-style cats, simply because this type of marking is present in many different species. The pattern may just look attractive to our eyes but it has a function for the cat—it breaks up the shape of its body and thus helps to conceal its presence.

developed the breed. The Singapura is the smallest domestic breed of cat and, although it still remains rare, its future seems relatively secure.

These small cats are quite social with each other, and seem to associate readily in groups. They are generally placid, and also tend to be very inquisitive by nature. They like company so they are not the ideal pet if you plan to spend long periods of the day away from home.

Wild Abyssinian And Ceylonese
The other breed that has descended over recent years from cats living semiwild in Singapore is the wild Abyssinian. Examples of this variety are now coming into the United States. It is also a ticked tabby breed, but unlike the Abyssinian itself, it retains tabby barring on the legs, with solid dark necklaces also evident around the neck. It appears to be a throwback to the ancestral form of the Abyssinian itself, which first became popular in Victorian Britain in the late 1800s before these areas of color were removed by selective breeding.

Meadow. Singapura is the Malaysian name for Singapore. These cats resembled Abyssinians with their ticked tabby appearance—from a combination of light and dark banding extending down each hair—but also have distinctive tabby barring on the inside of their legs and a dark tip to the tail. They exist in a single light color known as sepia, with pale ivory on the belly, chest, and lower face.

The Meadows obtained three felines and returned with them to the United States, where Tommy

Farther west in Asia, the island of Sri Lanka, which used to be called Ceylon, is home to the Ceylonese. These cats are virtually identical to the wild Abyssinian but typically display a more sandy gold coloration known as manila, although several other color variations are known. First introduced to Italy in 1984, the Ceylonese remains popular there, although the wild Abyssinian has tended to fade from the scene in the United States over recent years.

Family groups of these cats will again display a strong bond, reflecting the way in which they first lived in their homeland. They also have an very strong independent streak in their natures.

Sokoke Forest Cat

It is not just island populations of cats that display unusual color or coat variants. The Sokoke forest cat, which originated in Sokoke Arabuke forest on the coast of Kenya in eastern Africa, has a unique tabby patterning quite unlike that associated with other breeds. It is essentially a version of the classic blotched tabby pattern, but looks more like wood-graining. The coat is very short and shiny and lies close to the body. The lighter areas of the coat are a warm caramel and the darker markings vary from dark brown to almost black—there are no white hairs at all.

The first record of these cats dates back to 1977, when a litter of kittens was discovered in an area of forest being cleared. They were rescued and hand-reared, and then started to breed. Ultimately, some of these cats were sent to a Danish breeder, and they are now starting to appear elsewhere in Europe.

No one is sure about their origins—it is thought they may have been the result of a mutation occurring in cats that had strayed into this area, since the original kittens

A Cat's Tale
Tabby Patterns

There are four well-established tabby variants, although all such cats display a characteristic M-shaped or "scarab" marking on the head.

The oldest recorded form of tabby marking is the so-called classic, blotched, or oystershell pattern, which has stripes and is distinguishable by the presence of a black blotch on the flanks. Mackerel patterning consists of a series of stripes running down the sides of the body, rather like a fish's skeleton. In the case of the spotted tabby, the pattern of blotches, or stripes, is broken at regular intervals to create a series of spots. The ticked tabby is a subtle diffuse pattern—all the hairs are banded in alternate light and dark and there are no solid areas of color.

The Sokoke forest cat is a variant of the classic pattern—without the characteristic flank blotches, but with striped markings that are very similar to wood-graining.

were too friendly toward humans to be of true feral stock.

Lively and active, these cats are avid climbers, reflecting the wooded area in which the breed evolved. They are very affectionate, too, and not generally shy. Although they can be quite independent, they bond closely with their owner and can be very sensitive to human moods. Although still rare outside Denmark, they are gradually gaining in popularity.

Your Cat's
Sixth Sense

Largely nocturnal by nature and more

active as dusk falls, cats have gained a

reputation for being creatures of the

night—as well as familiar with other

lovers of darkness, such as witches and devils.

Cats who mysteriously find their way back home across

country to loved ones are also a well-recognized feline

phenomenon, but is this magical behavior paranormal, or

simply the cat using its instinctive navigational skills?

Cats And The Occult

People think that a cat's instinctive ability to identify the only person in the room who is not a cat lover is uncanny. The reason is actually very straightforward: as patient predators, cats are highly observant creatures and their action is based on our reactions. A cat is nervous about being stared at by strangers, since this is seen as threatening behavior, so she will tend to approach the person who does not look at her—and this is most likely someone who has no interest in or affection for cats! There may be a simple explanation in this case, but sometimes events seem to defy any rational scientific explanation, based on what we know and can surmise about cats. Your own pet's behavior may reflect true psychic powers.

One of the fascinating things about cats is their ability to disappear when they are allowed outside. In the past, they would venture out in search of food in the evening and might not be seen again until the following day. At a time when there was no widespread street lighting, even in

Although at night it may appear completely dark outside to us, cats are well-adapted to see in such conditions. Their nocturnal wandering explains many of the myths that have grown up around them.

major cities, darkness may have appeared much more menacing than it is today, which might have led to an assumed connection between cats and witchcraft.

Black cats in particular used to attract suspicion, simply because their color was linked with the dark forces of the devil. There are numerous local superstitions about what people could do to protect themselves. In the southwest English county of Cornwall, for example, there was once a belief that anyone out walking who met an unknown black cat should pause immediately and draw a cross on their shoe with the tip of a wet finger, to protect themselves from danger.

Much of the folklore surrounding the devil and his black cat messenger can be traced back to the building of bridges during medieval times. Constructing a successful bridge was a considerable feat and many believed that it involved a pact with the devil. One story tells of a French bishop, St. Cedo, who was horrified to learn that local people had entered into such a pact, offering the devil the soul of whoever crossed the bridge first. The bishop overcame the threat to his flock by ensuring that a black cat was first over the bridge, much to the devil's anger.

Cats were also associated with many pagan gods and goddesses. In the far north, for example, the fertility goddess Freya—from whose name comes the day of the week known as Friday—rode in a chariot drawn by cats. The felines represented the fecundity and the fierceness of the goddess. The Finns believed in a cat-drawn sledge that took away souls. Gradually the cat's role in pagan festivals led to a period of persecution that was to last for nearly 500 years.

Links between cats and magic exist in many cultures; cats are often believed to possess supernatural powers.

The way in which cats seem to disappear outside as darkness falls has sometimes led to suggestions that they can change their form.

In the past, the affinity that some cats display toward their owners has been misinterpreted as a sign of the occult.

Cats In Human Form

In the medieval period many believed in transmogrification—especially in the case of black cats. Witches were supposed to be able to adopt an animal form at will and subsequently change back again.

The mysterious habits of the cat—especially their way of becoming more active at dusk—meant that they were an obvious choice as a witch's familiar. Such a belief seems to have been widespread and can be traced back to Aesop's *Fables*, which were written some 2,000 years ago. Asian tales feature Neko-Bake, a magician

who adopts the shape of a cat to enter the homes of willful children and eat them. This was doubtless a story that many parents told their offspring to encourage good behavior!

In 1681 a French playwright, Regnard, wrote of magicians in Lapland and described how they transformed evil people into black cats. Another story from the Ozark Mountains in the United States tells of a man who accepts a bet to stay overnight in a house once occupied by witches. All is quiet until midnight, when the man is awoken by a huge cat. Reacting instinctively, he fires at the creature and then discovers a severed human foot on the table. The next day he is told that one of his neighbors has died, after shooting her foot off and hemorrhaging to death.

A number of similar tales emanate from France, where there was a very widespread acceptance that people could assume the shape of cats to carry out evil deeds. This belief was particularly strong in the vicinity of the Vosges Mountains, and has given rise to a number of local folktales.

A typical account features a man, Pichard, who regularly encounters a large white cat in a village square that he passes through on his way home after meeting his fiancée, Nanon. In due course the two lovers marry, life is good, and Pichard forgets about the cat completely. Then one night he sits up in bed with a start and realizes that Nanon has disappeared. The next morning his wife is back in bed and

A Cat's Tale
A Fishy Story

Not all such stories show the cat in a bad light—they may simply reveal that she has mystical powers. In one example, an Asian fish seller regularly leaves some extra scraps of fish for a rich customer's cat when he delivers the household order. Subsequently the fish seller falls very ill and is facing the collapse of his business. The cat assumes human form and takes the sick man two gold coins from her master's fortune, so the man soon recovers and once again his business prospers.

Calling on the wealthy man a few weeks later, the fish seller cannot see the cat and asks where she is. His customer explains that he has killed the animal, because he discovered that she had stolen some money. Immediately the fish seller realizes what has happened and tells his story. The cat's owner, racked with guilt, then constructs a temple to the memory of his pet.

he wonders if he had dreamed that she was missing—particularly as she denies that anything unusual has occurred. However, Pichard stays awake the following night and at midnight his wife goes missing again and he sees the large white cat from the square in the bedroom.

A Cat's Tale
The Cult Of Basht

After agriculture became widespread in the fertile Nile Valley, the stores of food began to attract rodents. Drawn by the ready availability of their natural prey, African wildcats soon began to visit settlements and were welcomed as an effective means of controlling the rodents. This mutually beneficial relationship marked the start of ancient Egypt's love affair with the cat, which ultimately saw her elevated to the role of a deity in the guise of goddess Basht, who was portrayed with the body of a woman and the head of a cat.

Basht was almost certainly a fertility goddess, and her cult entailed a gruesome ritual performed each spring, in which cats were killed and entombed in front of audiences of up to half a million onlookers. Based on archeological evidence, over 100,000 cats may have been sacrificed in this way. Although this ritual ended after about 2,000 years in 390 B.C. the legacies of it can still be seen in contemporary portrayals of cats today—not least the way in which cats are often represented with feminine characteristics. Also one of the alternative names for Basht was Pasht, which possibly become corrupted to "puss"—an affectionate name often used for cats.

By morning Nanon has returned, but Pichard is now determined to unravel the mystery. With the bedroom door firmly bolted he keeps watch and when he sees a white object touch the bolt he lashes at it with a hatchet; there is a terrible

Cats are often favored as companions by people living alone— especially the elderly. This once caused speculation that such people were witches.

scream, then silence. He finds Nanon has vanished again, but she returns after eight days and goes straight to bed—she is missing her hand, which has been chopped off at the wrist.

Beliefs of this type survived well into the eighteenth century. William Montgomery, a Scotsman who lived in Caithness, claimed he was plagued by cats around his home. One night, unable to bear the noise any longer, he rushed out with an axe, killed two cats, and wounded another. The next day two old women were discovered dead in their beds, while a third had an inexplicable wound to her leg.

Stories of marital infidelity that involve a cat probably stem from her nocturnal nature—she ventures out in search of mates at night. There are also numerous fertility cults that have been linked with cats at differing stages in history. Sasti, the Indian feline goddess, was a symbol of maternity, emphasizing the sexual potency of the cat. This may be a reflection of the overt sexual behavior of queens when they are ready to mate—they adopt a characteristic crouched position known as lordosis.

The persistent links between cats and the elderly may be harder to understand, but older people living alone do often keep cats as companions. Strange behavior by such older people may have scared others, especially children, giving rise to stories that they were witches who sought out the company of cats and preferred them to people.

Lucky Or Unlucky?

Cat are often secretive by nature, observing what is happening around them from a safe vantage point.

Many superstitions surround black cats; in some cultures they are considered lucky, in others as harbingers of ill-fortune.

In the United States and a number of countries across continental Europe, white cats are considered to be fortunate, while black cats bring bad luck. In Britain, the reverse situation applies—black cats are regarded as harbingers of good fortune. It is not necessary to own the cat to benefit from her power, you just have to see her cross in front of you. However, in some areas of England the way you greet the cat is also important—at least one local custom dictates that you must stroke her three times to benefit from the good luck.

If a black cat unexpectedly turns up at your home, superstition says she should never be turned away since this would bring bad luck. The same applies on boats.

Tortoiseshell cats are also often viewed as being lucky—not just in Britain, but also in Asia and Japan in particular. The presence of a cat in certain places is also sometimes considered to bring good fortune, especially if a cat makes her home in a theater. However, if the theater cat is kicked by an actor or chooses to run across the stage unexpectedly during a performance, she brings bad luck.

Cats As Protectors

In the past there were some cultures, such as those in the Far East, that believed cats had protective powers, perhaps because they were originally highly prized as an effective means of controlling rodents. In these areas of the world it became accepted practice to place a ceramic figure of a cat in the window to ward off poverty.

In medieval England, cats were often entombed in new buildings, sometimes along with a rat or with a single worn boot. The reason: to attract and trap any evil spirits or witches and guard the occupants of the house from harm. In eastern England, the mummified remains of a cat are sometimes found in wall spaces or under the roof thatch when renovation work is carried out. These days, rather than using a live cat, wooden or metal images of cats are often placed on the roofs of thatched homes instead.

Since settlers took the basic belief in a cat's protective powers abroad from England, variations on this practice have been also observed elsewhere in the world. In Australia, mummified cats are sometimes found in floor spaces, near the foundations, while in the United States they may be present in old chimneys. One of the oldest examples was discovered at the Terry-Mulford House in Orient, Long Island, New York.

Cats As Healers

Superstition often surrounded illness and cats have been perceived as possessing healing powers. Ancient folklore held that the tail of a black cat could be used to cure a stye in the

A Cat's Tale
Seasons And Character

It was once believed that the time of year when a kitten was born would affect its personality. Kittens born in May were thought to be sickly—and also dangerous, given to lying on top of babies and suffocating them. Such kittens were not expected to be good mousers and were blamed for encouraging snakes and slow-worms to venture into houses. In part this belief may have arisen because reptiles emerge from hibernation around this time of the year and would be seeking a warm spot in which to live.

In the southern English county of Sussex, young cats born after the festival of Michaelmas on October 11, were often known as blackberry kittens. They were regarded as being mischievous by nature, because there was a superstition that the Devil had fallen to earth at this time of year and ended up in a briar patch.

eye if the tail was rubbed across the affected area while an incantation was spoken. For the treatment to be successful the sex of the cat needed to be opposite to that of the person!

An instinctive ability to predict the weather could be advantageous for cats in the wild. This might be achieved to some extent by being able to detect changes in atmospheric pressure.

Warts could be made to disappear in a similar fashion, using a tortoiseshell cat but only during the month of May. A sick person who dreamed of cats fighting was doomed to die, and someone was also destined to die if the family pet abandoned the home and could not be persuaded to return.

Can Cats Predict The Weather?

Being able to sense weather changes would be a useful skill for wildcats—and an instinct that their domestic relatives may have inherited. Belief in a cat's ability to predict the weather was especially evident in fishing communities—perhaps because their work is so dependent on fine weather. There was also quite a widespread acceptance of this skill in France, with a range of different feline activities indicating various weather changes.

If a cat passed a paw behind an ear while grooming, there would soon be rain, while windy weather was indicated by a cat rubbing its nose, or running wildly about the home and digging its claws into cushions. Sneezing also indicated rain on the way—although there could be other meanings as well. On a bride's wedding day a cat sneezing once was a good omen for the future, but three sneezes in succession meant that everyone in the family would develop a cold. Fishing communities in the English county of Yorkshire believed that cats could influence the weather directly, rather than simply predicting it. Black cats were kept indoors while fishermen were away from home, otherwise storms were likely and the voyage could be very dangerous.

Even today, many owners are convinced that their cats can predict the approach of thunderstorms. Cats often display an inherent dislike of thunder and frequently show signs of distress as a storm approaches. They may become increasingly frantic and refuse to settle down, or they will try and find somewhere to hide. Some cats become much more aggressive and resent being handled. Cats can almost certainly sense the changes in atmosphere that precede a storm, and their acute hearing may also allow them to hear the sounds of approaching thunder well before it is audible to our ears.

This sensitivity may also explain the remarkable behavior displayed by some cats during World War II. When bombing raids were taking place over British towns and cities, a number of accounts tell of cats alerting their owners to impending danger even before the public air-raid warnings had sounded.

Typical is the story of Sally, a black-and-white cat who lived in the Docklands area in east London. Just before a raid she would start scratching at the gas mask hanging in the hall and running out to the air-raid shelter to paw at the door. Once her owner had safely

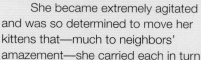

A Cat's Tale
Mother Knows Best

Unsurprisingly there are numerous stories of mother cats risking extreme danger to protect their kittens. The naval city of Plymouth, England, was heavily bombed during World War II, and an account from there tells of a female cat who had given birth and was left alone in the house.

She became extremely agitated and was so determined to move her kittens that—much to neighbors' amazement—she carried each in turn through a partially opened upper window and then walked along a telephone line some way above the ground. She took the same precarious route with each kitten, before depositing it safely in a nearby garden shed. Shortly afterward there was a bombing raid, and a large explosion rocked the area, badly damaging the house. The cat may well have heard the approach of the bombers, but how could she have known that her family was in danger—or was it just a lucky coincidence?

retreated to the shelter Sally would fetch the neighbor, only venturing into the shelter once she was sure they were both safe.

Interest in interpreting cat behavior is partly triggered by curiosity, but also stems from the widespread belief that cats possess greater insights into the world around us than we do.

Natural Disasters

There are a number of cases of cats apparently using some sixth sense to detect natural disasters. The Italian volcano Vesuvius had been quiet for over 80 years until a violent eruption on March 21, 1944.

That night a couple was asleep in their farmhouse, close to the town of San Sebastian, when their black-and-white cat Toto pawed at his owner's cheek and woke them both. Although he was ejected from the room, Toto returned and repeated his actions. This time the farmer's wife decided Toto was trying to warn them and she persuaded her husband to pack their belongings into a cart and head away from the volcano to his sister-in-law's house. Less than an hour later the eruption occurred, killing 30 people, wrecking the town, and leaving more than 5,000 people homeless.

In May 1976, local people in the region around Friuli, in northeastern Italy, noted their cats were behaving strangely, rushing around their homes and trying to escape outdoors. In three separate cases, queens dragged their kittens outside and left them in the bushes. Not long afterward a significant earthquake rocked the area. It is not just cats that behave in this uncanny way—other creatures do, too. For example, many animals showed a widespread and urgent desire to vacate the area of Haicheng in central China in 1943, which led the authorities to insist that the townsfolk also abandon their homes.

The following day a huge earthquake caused widespread devastation, but many lives were saved thanks to the behavior of the animals. More recently it seems that few domestic animals died in the dreadful Pacific tsunami that struck on December 26, 2004, which once again indicates that they sensed the peril beforehand and made it safely to higher ground.

How cats can detect impending danger remains unclear, although there is serious scientific interest in studying this behavior to see if it could provide an early warning in areas of greatest risk. One leading investigator, Dr. Helmut Tributsch— an Italian from the area of Friuli—has

Evidence during recent events—from volcanic eruptions to tsunamis— seems to show that cats are more sensitive to impending natural disasters than humans.

suggested it may be linked to the increasing number of positive ions that are released into the atmosphere prior to an earthquake. The same phenomenon occurs on a smaller scale before the arrival of a storm.

We can also sense such changes—but while we might simply develop a slight headache, cats respond in a more dramatic fashion. It is possible that the level of chemical messengers in the cat's brain is directly affected, thus altering its pattern of behavior.

Cats' superior hearing may also play a part because they can hear sounds of a much higher frequency than we can. There is the interesting case of Barney, a ginger tom who slept every night on top of the family's cathode ray tube television. One night he woke suddenly and dashed out of the room; soon afterward the tube exploded, which would have caused a serious injury to the cat if he had been asleep as normal. It seems most likely that Barney was woken up by a noise from the tube that was inaudible to his owner. Cats near the epicenter of an earthquake may well hear the sounds of early minor tremors. When

The cat's highly tuned senses help it to locate prey—and perhaps also to avoid some dangers.

these tremors are combined with a significant rise in positively charged particles in the atmosphere, the cat may receive an early warning of impending disaster. There may even be a third factor, when such events lead to changes in the earth's magnetic field. It is believed cats and other creatures use the magnetic field to orient themselves, see page 161.

Cats As Lifesavers

There are a surprising number of cases of cats that save people's lives through their actions—although usually linked with the feline's own desire to escape from danger.

However, cats can also be selfless on occasion, too. One account concerns a stray cat almost dying from hypothermia that turned up on the porch of Virgil and Linda McMillian's house in Berryville, Arkansas, on a freezing night. The couple took him in and nursed him back to health, and he became a much-loved pet they named Slowly Cat. Each night, he was put outside for a few minutes before the couple went to bed, but he always returned to the house very quickly.

They were therefore very alarmed when he vanished one night two years later, especially as the temperature began to fall well below freezing. They searched everywhere around their property without success, and the following morning there was still no sign of him. Fearing the worst, the couple began looking again in daylight and Virgil spotted an old burlap sack lying on the ground. Slowly Cat slowly emerged from within, but then unexpectedly crawled back inside again. Virgil opened the sack and was

Test Your Cat's Psychic Powers

There are a couple of tests that you can carry out to see how close your bond is with your cat. It helps if you are relaxed when carrying out these tests.

Wait until your pet is asleep, then sit nearby in the room and stare intently at her for perhaps 30 seconds at a time, concentrating on an image of your cat with you. This should lead to your cat waking up and coming to sit alongside you. If nothing happens, try again after a minute or so.

When you are sitting or lying down, free from any other distractions, try calling your cat to come to you through your mind's eye. You will need to concentrate very intently on your pet, so you could

try reinforcing her image by studying a photograph of you both together. She will probably appear in no time by your side.

Cats On The Move

Cat owners who move from a home are often amazed to discover that their pet has returned to former haunts—although usually this entails a journey of just a few miles. In 1960, however, a cat called McCavity made headlines when he undertook a marathon trek back to Cumbernauld, near Glasgow in Scotland, from his new home close to Truro in Cornwall in the far southwest of England—covering the distance of about 500 miles (800 km) in only three weeks. Sadly, McCavity was so weakened by his effort that he died soon afterward, but cats can undertake longer journeys of this type and remain in good health—after all, they cover large territories in the wild.

Animals from sea turtles to swallows can find the way back to their birthplace over thousands of miles, using the Earth's magnetic fields. This helps to provide a clue to journeys such as that undertaken by McCavity. The first experiment into a cat's ability to find its way home was carried out in 1921 by Professor Francis H. Herrick, who drove his cat to a spot about 5 miles (8 km) from his home in Cleveland, Ohio, and let her try and find her own way back. The professor finally arrived home

Cats such as this young kitten (above) will soon orient themselves in a new home, recognizing familiar landmarks so they will not get lost if they are allowed to roam outdoors.

amazed and horrified to find a tiny baby inside, clearly very near death. Slowly Cat lay next to him, licking his face. The baby was rushed to hospital, where his body temperature had fallen to just 94 degrees.

Doctors were convinced that without the warmth provided by the McMillians' cat throughout the night, the infant would not have survived. So what drew Slowly Cat to the sack, and why did he stay with the baby all night? Male cats do not have the maternal instincts of females, so the only explanation would appear to be that Slowly Cat remembered being rescued from freezing in very similar circumstances. Perhaps he was conditioned to behave in the way he did because of the care and attention lavished upon him by the McMillians.

There is no evidence that any particular breed of cat—including non-pedigree felines—has a stronger homing instinct than others. However, Persians are popularly believed to stay closer to home than other cats.

considerably more exhausted than his pet, having followed the cat on foot as she took the most direct route home across fields and through hedges, leaping small obstacles in her path.

Over 200 cases of cats traveling long distances have now been studied, and it appears that a cat will walk around 3 miles (5 km) each day on average on such a journey, usually pausing to hunt on the way. It is believed that they rely initially on the Earth's magnetic field to orient themselves and head off in the right general direction, then switch to looking for familiar landmarks, and finally sniff out the route as they get close to their destination.

Cats regularly mark their territories with their scent and are known to have a very keen sense of smell. What is much harder to explain

is how a cat such as Sugar (see box below left, *The Case Of Sugar*) can set off into the unknown and manage to find people a long distance away in a totally strange area. Scenting skills would appear to be of little value in this case, nor are there any other obvious points of guidance that a cat could use. In fact we simply do not understand how this journey could be achieved and some scientists have suggested that cats possess a form of extrasensory perception that enables them to reach their destination.

Such a journey also requires deliberate choice by the cat—after all, it would have been simpler for Sugar to stay with his new owners than to embark on an arduous and hazardous journey into unknown terrain. A cat's determination to return to its owner suggests that our cats can become just as attached to us as we are to them!

A Cat's Tale
The Case Of Sugar

When Mr. and Mrs. Woods moved from California to Oklahoma in 1951, they decided to leave their cat Sugar behind with a neighbor because he was terrified of traveling and their move entailed a journey of about 1,500 miles (2,400 km). It was roughly a year later when a cat resembling Sugar unexpectedly jumped directly on to Mrs. Woods' shoulder in the backyard of her new home. Although struck by the amazing similarity, she did not think that it could possibly be Sugar until she noticed the distinctive deformity of his left hip joint when stroking him. Checking back with her friends in California, Mrs. Woods discovered that Sugar had left his new home shortly after she and her husband had moved away and he had not been seen there since. How Sugar was able to track down the Woods over such a distance and in a strange area is a remarkable mystery.

Ghost Cats

The character of the grinning Cheshire Cat, immortalized in the famous children's book *Alice in Wonderland* probably has a basis in a ghostly tale about a cat—especially because author Lewis Carroll lived in in the English county of Cheshire and had an interest in psychic research.

The original story dates from the early 1800s, when two women visiting the remains of an ancient abbey near Congleton, Cheshire, noticed a striking white cat. As they approached the creature it vanished suddenly and although they searched briefly they couldn't find it.

On another visit, the same thing happened. The couple recounted their story of the strange disappearing cat and learned that he had been kept locally by a Mrs. Winge but had disappeared many years beforehand, leaving his owner worried that her pet had been killed. However, some time later she heard him scratching at the door to come in—but he would never set foot inside the home again, simply disappearing in front of his owner's eyes. Many other people in the neighborhood had also encountered this ghostly creature.

There are numerous other less well-known cases of cats reappearing to owners after their deaths, usually in the familiar locations they had favored in the home. This may sometimes be explained by the mind's eye projecting the image of the cat from memory, because the owner has seen the cat sleeping here on so many occasions in the past. Especially interesting are those cases in which the person has acquired another cat after the death of the first and she reacts in her new home as if she has seen a ghost as well. However, with her acute sense of smell, she may be detecting the scent of the home's former occupant, particularly if the cat's bedding has not been washed or the carpeting in the house cleaned thoroughly since the first cat's death.

There are various well-documented cases of human ghosts—and there are also a number of similar accounts of feline apparitions.

Cat
Behavior
A–Z

Domestic cats remain opportunistic, even stealing food although they no longer need to catch their own prey. Although some behavior is instinctive, more infantile traits are a result of their dependency on us. Understanding why your cat behaves in a particular way is not only interesting, it will improve communication with your pet, and strengthen the bond between you. Being aware of your cat's normal behavior also enables you to spot if there is something wrong at an early stage.

A

Avoiding Your Glare

Cats are sensitive, and can quickly pick up on their owner's moods and their tone of voice. As a result, your pet will soon realize if you are displeased, and will seek to avoid your gaze. This is because staring directly at another cat in a potential conflict situation is perceived as a challenge, so your cat is instinctively deflecting your anger by looking elsewhere.

B

Being Sick

Vomiting is normally caused by a fur ball in the stomach. The cat's tongue has backward pointing projections, called papillae, which give it a rough surface. As the cat grooms itself, this "natural brush" will remove loose fur from the coat but the cat may find it difficult to remove the hairs, so they are often swallowed. They can form a solid pad in the stomach, known either as a fur ball or hairball. The first signs of this obstruction may be a change in your pet's appetite because the mass of fur in her stomach restricts how much she can eat at any one time. Whereas she may have eaten a reasonable amount of food at each meal, she now picks at her food, eating only a small amount but returning to eat more. You may think she has become bored with what is offered, but if you take the food bowl away, your cat will pester you for more food and will seem constantly hungry.

A laxative to help free the blockage may solve this problem. The traditional treatment is to add about 1 tsp. (5 ml) of mineral oil (also known as liquid paraffin), which is sold in drugstores, to the cat's food for two days. If this fails, an operation to remove the blockage may be necessary.

If you know your cat is susceptible to fur balls, be sure to groom her every day—especially during molting season—to ensure that she does not have an opportunity to swallow loose hairs. You can also try switching to a commercial cat food mixtures containing ingredients to help prevent fur balls from forming.

If you notice that your cat is eating grass, it is usually a sign that she is about to be sick. Occasionally, vomiting is a sign of a build-up of intestinal worms, with the grass acting as an emetic. If you think your cat may have worms, you will need to give her a worming tablet to clear them from her system. Worming tablets are available from pet supply stores or from your vet.

Cats can also be sick as the result of an infection, so if your pet looks generally ill and is vomiting, arrange to take her to your vet without delay, so an appropriate treatment can be given. *See also: Grass Eating.*

Birth

If your cat is about to give birth, she may appear restless, refuse to eat, meow a great deal, or pace up and down. All this is normal behavior and is no cause for alarm. A healthy cat is unlikely to have any problems during delivery and it is important that you interfere as little as possible. Call your vet if your cat bleeds excessively—more than 2 tsp. (10 ml)—if the contractions go on for more than an hour with no kitten being delivered, or if a kitten is partially delivered but then appears to become stuck.

After delivery, the mother will probably not eat or drink for a day or two, but after that she will need constant access to her usual food and fresh, clean water. Contact your vet if she appears to be lethargic, fails to eat or drink after a few days, has a fever, or ignores her kittens.

Do not handle the kittens for the first week, but after the second week they should be picked up regularly so they will learn to socialize with humans properly.

Kittens will feed around three times an hour at first, but if they cry constantly and appear hungry, the mother may not be producing enough milk. Contact your vet for advice on hand-feeding. *See also: Disappearing Kittens.*

C

Clawing

Many cats have an unfortunate habit of digging their claws into the cover of a chair and even your lap before sitting down. This is likely to damage the chair cover or your clothing, and be painful too, because your cat flexes its paws as she does so, curling her claws round as a result. Such behavior stems from kittenhood, with these movements used by the kitten to express milk from its mother's teat. As a result, it can be difficult to correct effectively. You may have to rely on a wrap thrown over the chair or your lap to minimize the risk of injury or damage.

Some North American owners resort to having their cats declawed, which involves an operation called onychectomy. This procedure is not permitted in many countries such as the United Kingdom, because it is regarded as imposing a constraint on the cat's natural

behavior. Cats that have lost their claws may not be able to groom themselves as effectively, or climb to escape danger or defend themselves in a fight if they are in danger outdoors. This surgery is usually something that is carried out for an owner's convenience, rather than aiding their pet. *See also: Scratching Furniture; Scratching You.*

Crying

Cats' eyes are bathed in a special tear fluid to keep the surfaces moist, and there is a drainage hole in each eye that carries excess fluid out of the eyes. If your cat is very tolerant, you may be able to spot these by rolling down one of her lower eyelids slightly. It is a tiny opening, located a short distance away from the nose. The fluid that flows through here enters the nasolacrimal duct and passes down into the nose.

In the case of cats with relatively flat faces, such as Persian longhairs, these ducts can become distorted and obstruct the flow of the tear fluid. It then runs out of the eye directly, making it look as if your cat is crying. The situation often becomes worse in cold weather, simply because the outflow of tear fluid is greater at this stage. Aside from wiping away the tear deposits where they form below each eye, the only long-term solution may be for your vet to operate to improve the drainage from the eyes.

D

Dashing Around

Cats that spend much of their time indoors will occasionally launch into sudden, wild dashes around the home, especially in the case of young felines. These may be a way of burning off surplus energy, mimicking how cats often sprint after prey outdoors. You may even be able to predict when

A Cat's Tale
Upwardly Mobile

Certain breeds—particularly Siamese and the Orientals—will not only dash madly about on the ground but may also try to climb the window drapes. They often cause considerable damage with their claws, so try to keep drapes out of their reach.

your cat is likely to behave this way. This behavior may stem from a game of chase, particularly if your cat becomes bored. Such behavior rarely causes any harm, provided your cat does not knock over any household items. You may find that as your cat grows older, she is less inclined to behave this way. Beware of trying to handle her while she is in this mood though, because you could easily end up getting a bad scratch.

Digging

Cats that roam outdoors will usually seek out different areas of their territory to deposit their feces, which, unlike their larger wild relatives, they will bury in the ground. Therefore, not surprisingly, they are generally on the lookout for soft earth that will make this job easier. Freshly dug soil is especially appealing to them. This can be very irritating to gardeners though, because it often results in newly planted bulbs or young plants being dug up.

This behavior can create ill feelings with your neighbors, although there is little that you can do to prevent your cat from roaming and behaving in this way if she is outdoors, unless you erect a cat-proof fence around your garden. These are now available from pet supply companies, and are often advertised in cat magazines or through the Internet; they will help to keep your pet safe from traffic, too.

If you are determined to keep your cat out of your flower beds, then after digging you will probably need to cover the area with plastic bird netting. There are also various treatments that you can sprinkle around the perimeter of the bed, which may help to deter your pet from entering this area. However, often their effectiveness is seriously reduced when it rains, and not all work well in the first place either—although they should not harm your pet in any event.

If there is a particular area that you want to deter your cat from walking across on a regular basis, try planting the herb known as rue (*Ruta graveolens*) in this area. It is an ancient means of deterring cats, recommended by Roman writers.

Disappearing Kittens

Young cats are very vulnerable to predators, so a female cat in the wild usually has several locations where she can move her kittens, carrying each one gently in her mouth by the scruff of the neck between locations. Be careful if your queen has kittens in the home. She may seek to move them outdoors, particularly if she feels insecure. This is why it is important for younger members of the family not to disturb her unnecessarily, especially while the kittens are still very young, because this can be upsetting for the mother.

Dribbling

Cats may dribble after being treated with a flea powder that has stimulated a flow of saliva, but the most common reason for this behavior is an underlying dental problem. In close proximity, you may notice that your cat's breath has an unpleasant odor. If you watch her eat—particularly if you are feeding her dry food—you may see that she nibbles it rather cautiously because of an underlying pain associated with her teeth. You may need to have your cat's teeth treated by your vet to resolve this problem. You can try to prevent dental problems by brushing your cat's teeth—if she will let you—using a specially-formulated pet toothpaste and brush, available from pet supply stores. Never use human toothpaste, which has ingredients that can upset a cat's stomach.

A Cat's Tale
On The Move

A female cat with kittens can be very determined to move her litter. Do not assume that she will only try to use the door—if this is closed, she may decide to carry the kittens through an open window. Be sure the room she is in is safe and secure, and watch for any sign of the mother being uneasy.

Drinking Behavior

Water is very important for cats, particularly those eating dry food, because they receive much less fluid as part of their normal food intake compared with cats fed wet food. Your cat should always have access to a bowl of fresh water, but often cats can be seemingly perverse, and you may notice that your pet walks past the water bowl, and goes outside to drink from a puddle or a garden pond. It might be that she simply prefers the taste of standing water, although cats do not usually avoid water fresh from the tap. Clearly though, it will be much better if she drinks water indoors because of the risk that she may consume polluted water elsewhere.

It will be even more hazardous for her health if your cat can gain access to antifreeze, which is used to prevent the water in car radiators from freezing in cold weather. Even though it contains a potentially deadly chemical called ethylene glycol, cats will readily drink antifreeze. Vomiting is an early sign of most types of poisoning, along with increased thirst—and there are likely to be several neurological signs, too. The main damage from antifreeze occurs in the kidneys however, and it is very important to seek veterinary advice as soon as possible, to help your pet survive. *See also: Being Sick.*

F

Fear Of Water

There is a widespread belief that all cats dislike water, but some wild cats will often enter water to hunt. Many domestic cats may stick a paw in a pond in hopes of catching a fish or frog, while the Turkish Van readily swims. Cats that are used to going in water from an early age have no fear of it, but if you suddenly have to try to bathe an older cat, you can face a surprising problem, when your normally docile pet begins spitting and scratching. Cats rarely need bathing though, compared to dogs, because they do not develop a distinctive body odor. Modern methods of preventive parasite control of parasites, such as for fleas, mean that bathing is likely to be unnecessary.

Show cats may sometimes need to be bathed however, so it is useful to accustom kittens to this experience. Try to reassure your pet as much as possible by standing your kitten in a bowl that contains a small amount of tepid water. Ladle the water out onto your cat's legs first, moving up to the sides of her body, and then gently move up toward the back. As you approach the cat's head, take particular care not to let water run down over the face because this may be very upsetting for your pet. If you need to clean this part of the body, it is usually better to do it with an old washcloth, just wiping it over your pet's head.

Always seek to reassure your pet, and if she becomes very distressed, do not continue. Try again several weeks later, when your cat may be more relaxed. If you persist, a bad experience may stay with her for life, making it difficult to bathe her again in the future. Gentle persuasion is the best way forward. Afterward, wrap her in a towel, and dry off her coat. Be very careful if you decide to use a hair dryer. Keep it on a cool setting so it will not be uncomfortable for your pet. Even so, many cats simply dislike the noise of a hair dryer at close quarters, and will try to run away, so you may have to be patient with your pet.

G

Grass Eating

Sometimes cats will eat grass, especially relatively long but not very coarse stems. This may mimic the way cats in the wild eat the stomach contents of their vegetarian prey, but it also adds fiber to your pet's diet. Eating grass may also serve as a natural remedy to help the cat vomit up a fur ball, or intestinal worms.

Although grass is not essential to your cat's well-being, you should offer it to see if she wants to eat it. If you have a house cat, it is very easy to provide a fresh supply of grass by growing it on a windowsill. Simply place this in an area where your cat likes to sit, so she can nibble at it. Keep it adequately watered, and you will find that it lasts for some weeks, particularly if you cut it back with scissors, if necessary, to encourage fresh growth.

H

Hunting

Cats will hunt instinctively, but they need to learn how to kill prey effectively. Female cats frequently bring live, but maimed, prey back for their offspring to kill for this reason. Most pet cats, especially purebreds, have not learned how to do this, so they appear to torment their prey rather than killing it quickly. An experienced cat relies on her sharp canine teeth to inflict a deadly bite on her prey, normally in the neck region.

The fact that a cat hunts does not necessarily mean that she is hungry. In a garden setting, most cats are forced to hunt birds, rather than rodents which are their preferred prey and easier

for them to catch. Young cats tend to be the most active hunters; they lose interest in hunting once the prey becomes harder to catch as they grow older and less agile.

Unfortunately, it can be hard to deter a cat from hunting, other than by fitting your pet with an elastic collar with a bell attached. Most cats soon adapt to this however, and move stealthily to avoid ringing the bell until the last moment—so the benefits to the local wildlife population are only temporary. Cats will also hunt amphibians, and while frogs may be a relatively easy target, the impact of catching a toad can be much more severe. Toads are protected by toxic skin secretions that are likely to cause your pet to start foaming at the mouth.

L

Licking

A female cat will lick her kittens from birth, while older cats that know each other well will also groom each other in this fashion when they are relaxed. Some cats respond to their owner's attention in this way, usually licking a hand when you have been making a fuss of your pet. Not all cats behave this way though, but if your cat does,

you will notice the very rough surface of the cat's tongue on your skin. This is caused by tiny projections, known as papillae, which enable a cat to rasp meat off a bone, and pull any loose hair out of its coat.

Unfortunately it is very hard for a cat to spit out the hair that is caught in its mouth, so it is likely to be swallowed and lead to the formation of a fur ball in the stomach. This can cause a partial blockage, as well as reducing the volume of the stomach so that the cat starts to pick at its food because it cannot swallow large amounts.

Some cats will groom themselves excessively when they are under stress and feel threatened. Excessive licking can also be an indication of a food intolerance or allergy. In this case, try switching to a different diet, but do so gradually because not all cats will readily switch foods. Slowly increase the percentage of new food while reducing the amount of the cat's previous food over the course of a couple of weeks.

It is possible to obtain special hypoallergenic foods from some pet supply stores or a vet. These usually contain sources of protein such as duck or venison, rather than beef or chicken. If the symptoms improve, it is likely that the source of the problem was in your cat's diet.
See also: Being Sick.

A Cat's Tale
Painful Eating

Dental problems, such as loose teeth, may make eating painful and have an adverse effect on your pet's appetite— particularly in older cats. Fur balls can also turn a cat with a healthy appetite into a fussy eater.

Loss Of Appetite

There are a number of possible reasons for a cat to lose its appetite. The most common is illness. This may be a generalized infection, or possibly a problem localized to the mouth, such as painful teeth. The cat's third eyelid, at the corner of the eye, is often linked with illness. It appears as a pink membrane that extends over the surface of the eyeball from the corner. This occurs because the cat's body uses some of the fat surrounding the eyeballs in the absence of food, causing the eyes to sink back into their sockets. In any event, a veterinary checkup is recommended under these circumstances.

A sudden change in food may also impact your cat's appetite. This is why it is important to mix foods together, rather than switching rapidly, especially from wet food to dry food, which will be less palatable for a cat. In addition, if your cat has just suffered from an upset stomach, she is unlikely to eat the same food as before. A new food will help rekindle her appetite, and then you can go back to the previous type of food after about two months; by this time the cat's initial reluctance to eat it will have faded again.

Occasionally, environmental factors may impact your cat's appetite, too. A severe shock can sometimes have this effect, such as after a thunderstorm storm or fireworks, or following a fight. Changes in the cat's surroundings may also cause your pet to lose her appetite. This often happens, for example, if you have had builders creating a lot of noise, or introduced another cat or a dog to your home. Loss of appetite for these reasons will be temporary though, and can often be overcome by placing your cat in a quiet part of the home on her own, along with her food.

M

Messy Feeding Habits

It is always a good idea to break up the contents of a can of cat food with a knife into small pieces. This will encourage your pet to eat it in her bowl, rather than dragging it out onto the floor. Fresh food also should be cut into easy bite-sized pieces for the same reason. As an additional precaution, you may want to add a mat beneath, which will make it easy to mop up any food spills. You are unlikely to have this problem with dry food, simply because the kibbles form small pieces that your cat can pick up and swallow easily.

Cats behave this way because of the size of the food. They do not use the incisor teeth at the front of the mouth to nibble off small pieces. Instead, they have to rely on the carnassial teeth, which are located almost midway along their jaws for this purpose. This also means that they have to pull a large piece of food out of the food bowl, so they can hold it in this part of their jaws and slice it into smaller pieces which they can then swallow.

N

Noisy Cats

Some cat breeds are much more vocal than others; Siamese and related Oriental breeds are

the most vocal. The loud calls made by female cats in search of mates are much louder, and sound eerie after dark. The most ear-piercing calls are uttered by queens after mating however, when the tom cat withdraws from the female's body. This is because of the pain caused by the barbs on the tip of his penis, which rub against the walls of her vagina.

It is an essential and unavoidable part of the breeding cycle, because it is this pain that triggers the ovulation of the female, resulting in the release of eggs from her ovaries. Queens do not have a fixed breeding cycle. As solitary animals, they will only ovulate after mating, which increases the chances that they will become pregnant as a result.

The female's scream at this stage also serves as a warning to her partner—he needs to move away quickly, or she will lash out aggressively toward him. The effect of this trauma is temporary, because a queen may mate with several partners over the course of a single night, and may ultimately give birth to kittens sired by different toms in the same litter as a result.

P

Posturing

It is not unusual for cats to arch their backs when they are under threat, moving sideways. This is a way to intimidate their rival, without launching into a overtly aggressive response. The aim is to appear larger and fiercer and encourage their would-be opponent to back down. This type of behavior is usually accompanied by hissing and spitting. The cat also draws back its lips to reveal sharp canine teeth to reinforce its message.

There will be a number of other signs that indicate your cat's moods. Look at her ears. If they are upright, but pointing slightly forward, this is a sign that she is relaxed and confident. But if she is nervous, she will draw her ears back slightly, although they will still be raised. When a cat is hissing angrily, the ears are held further back, and flattened. If a fight breaks out, the ears are clamped tightly on the sides of the head, so they will be less exposed to injury. Nevertheless, it is common for toms who fight regularly to have torn and damaged ears.

A cat's pupils are not just affected by the prevailing light conditions, narrowing down to a slit in bright light, but they also change in respect

of its mood. At rest, a cat's pupils are normally round, but in an aggressive situation, they are likely to become significantly smaller.

R

Rolling Over

Young kittens will often roll over on their backs because this is a usual posture for periods of play with their littermates. Older cats may be much more reluctant to behave this way because they feel vulnerable in this position.

Your cat may roll over and then once you start stroking her chest and her belly, she may suddenly and unexpectedly kick out with her hind legs and scratch your hand unless you pull it away very quickly. She may also leap up quickly and withdraw from you.

Although this is very distressing, you need to respect your cat's limits in this case. When she rolls over again in this manner, simply restrict yourself to stroking her chest, rather than moving down her abdomen, because this is less likely to trigger such a violent reaction. On the other hand, if she is used to being stroked this way since kittenhood, you will probably not encounter this problem anyway.

S

Scratching Furniture

Cats scratch furniture for two reasons. First, they need to keep their front claws sharp, and scratching on a wooden surface is useful for this purpose. Second, scratching provides a form of exercise, helping to tone up the body, while it also serves as a territorial marker. The indelible impressions left by a cat's claws are a visual sign of its territorial claim, as is the scent from glands on its feet that is left at the same time.

To deter your cat from behaving this way toward your furniture, it is a good idea to invest in a scratching post. If you gently rub your cat's front paws down the post, she will soon recognize its purpose. You should also protect any areas of furniture that your cat may be inclined to scratch. This may also include the arms of sofas, rather than just the bare wood of chairs.

Scratching You

Cats are capable of inflicting very painful wounds with their claws. This can make them very difficult to handle, especially in the case of larger breeds, because they can use their hind legs very effectively. In order to avoid this problem, it is very important to accustom a young cat to being picked up regularly. This can be achieved more easily at this stage, while your cat is still relatively small because larger breeds, such as the Maine coon, can be a handful to lift up.

The most important thing to do to make your cat feel secure when she is picked up, is to be sure that you always support her hindquarters. Otherwise, if these hang down, you are likely to find that she will struggle, and this will cause her to lash out with her claws and scratch you. The simplest way to support your cat is to use your right hand to support her chest, and tuck her body in against yours if you are carrying her. When you put her down again, bend down to put her back on the ground, rather than encouraging her to jump down, as she could end up caught in your clothing as a result.

Children are often at the greatest risk of being scratched by a cat, simply because they may have difficulty in picking up the cat properly, and supporting its weight. Always teach your children how to pick up a pet properly to minimize this risk, although try to discourage them from doing so when you are not around. You also need to stress that a cat must not be teased during a game, or handled roughly, because this may cause her to lash out with her claws.

You are most likely to be scratched if you need to restrain your cat closely in order to give her a tablet, for example. Again, it is important to teach your cat to allow you to open her mouth from an early age, so that she will be less likely to be frightened by this experience once she grows older. Always sit your cat down on a level surface at a convenient height when you need to open her mouth, and if you are uncertain about how she will react, it may be advisable to wrap her in a thick blanket or towel. It will then be much harder for her to use her claws to scratch you. If she is frightened she may wriggle ferociously, but if she does break free she will be less likely to scratch you. However, it will be very difficult to approach her for a time afterward.

More worrisome, however, is the way some cats will lash out with no warning, in a non-confrontational situation, even when you are simply petting her. Be wary if you are making a fuss of a cat that you do not know well, just in case she lashes out suddenly and unexpectedly. It may be that you touched a painful area of her body, possibly where she might have been bitten recently in a fight. Alternatively, perhaps you moved your hand too quickly, which she then misinterpreted as an aggressive gesture. The cat may also recall being handled roughly in the past,

particularly if it has been held by the scruff of its neck at any stage.

Try to recall which part of your pet's body you were stroking when you were attacked. You may want to see cautiously whether it evokes a similar response again, in which case, even if you cannot identify the cause, you can avoid the risk area in the future.

Unfortunately, there are a few cats, typically felines that are relatively high strung, that will react this way for no obvious reason and without warning. There is little point in scolding your pet, because this will not have a lasting effect, and may only weaken the bond between you over the long term. Never react by hitting your cat if she does suddenly lash out and scratch your hand. This will cause her to become fearful of your hand rather than correcting the problem.

Self-Grooming

Cats are actually very fastidious about cleaning themselves. They have a regular grooming ritual, which is why you will need to clean your pet's coat if it has been soiled. Otherwise, cats are at risk of being poisoned if they lick their coat and ingest a substance contaminating their fur. This can lead to painful blistering of the tongue or more general signs of poisoning, such as a sudden difficulty in

A Cat's Tale
Hair Markers

Cats also often shed any loose fur as they move through their territory. When they squeeze through a gap, some strands of hair can be left behind on fencing or bushes. This will indicate to other cats in the area that they have passed through—in the same way as scent marking.

breathing, which can lead to collapse and death. Cats like to lie in warm spots, and may choose to lie on a driveway, for example, where there may be oil deposits. If you suspect poisoning, you need to contact your vet immediately for advice. The most appropriate treatment depends very much on the substance that has been swallowed.

Grooming is an instinctive behavior in cats, but they will also use it for what is known as displacement activity. If your cat is nervous or feels threatened, but is not sure how to react, she is likely to begin a grooming ritual. The only difference in this case is that it is likely to be carried out more rapidly than normal, reflecting the tension that she is feeling. It is a pacifying gesture, with your cat trying to convey an

impression that everything is normal, and indicate that she is relaxed, although in reality this is not the case.

In this situation, a cat is most likely to be concentrating on grooming her face with her front paws. The reason for this is simple—not only does it mean that she can avoid eye control, which could be perceived as a threat, but it also ensures that if necessary, she will be able to run off easily. If she was lying down, grooming the coat on the sides of her body, then this would not be possible and it would place her at a serious disadvantage if she was suddenly attacked.

There is evidence that some cats may even overgroom themselves because they are more nervous than usual. This is unlikely to cause any serious harm, but you should try to deal with the problem. Bach Flower Remedies sometimes prove useful.

The cat's grooming ritual is not carried out for vanity though. It is essential to your pet's well-being, and you are likely to notice that your cat grooms herself more when the weather is hot. This is quite usual, simply because cats cannot sweat to lose their body heat, the way that we do. Instead the cat leaves saliva on its fur. This utilizes body heat as it evaporates and keeps the body cooler as a result. In cold weather, licking the coat is also valuable, because this flattens the hair and forms a barrier. This traps warm air next to the skin and helps to maintain the cat's body temperature and keep her warm.

Cats start by cleaning the area around their face, before moving behind their ears, using their paws for this purpose. All cats follow a similar method of grooming, working back along their body with the tail always being groomed last. They groom areas of the body that they can reach directly, such as their underparts, by licking with their tongue, and this can leave them at risk of fur

balls. Loose hair is pulled out and sticks to the surface of the tongue with the risk that it will then be swallowed, and ultimately accumulate in the stomach.
See also: Being Sick.

Shaking Of The Head
Always be suspicious if your cat starts shaking her head, particularly if she starts pawing at the ears. It may be that she has a foreign body in the ear canal but, more commonly, this behavior is a sign of an ear infection, which will require veterinary treatment. Infections of this type can result from bacteria, fungi, ear mites, or a combination of all three, and it is important to determine the cause at the outset.

Sleeping Strangely
Cats sleep for relatively long periods each day, and studies of their sleep patterns reveal that like us, when they first fall asleep they enter a phase known as light sleep—usually being curled up at this stage. After as long as half an hour, the cat will then relax and may shift position, sometimes stretching out, and moving from a light phase of sleep—when your pet is most easily awoken— through to a deep sleep pattern. This is known as Rapid Eye Movement (REM) sleep, because of the way in which the eyes, although closed, start to move.

A more obvious indicator of REM sleep is the way in which a cat starts to twitch during this phase. This behavior is quite normal, with periods of this type lasting for about six minutes on average. It is followed by another period of light sleep, until the cat wakes up again. Your cat may be dreaming during these periods, absorbing information about her environment, just as we do in deep sleep. It is not a signs of epilepsy or any other underlying health problem.

Do not worry if your cat sleeps at a funny angle, even lying partly over the edge of a chair. Cats often prefer to sleep in small, confined spaces, as reflected in the past by ships' cats, which would frequently seek out hidden nooks as sleeping areas on voyages. This also corresponds to the small, snug dens favored by their wild ancestors.

Soiling Indoors

There are several behavioral and medical reasons that may underlie a breakdown in cleanliness on the part of your pet in the home. Cats actually use both their urine and feces for communication purposes, particularly in terms of asserting territorial claims. So it is not surprising that the introduction of a new cat to your home alongside your existing pet may lead to a breakdown in housecleanliness. It can be a difficult problem to overcome, but the best thing to do is to clean up using a descenting preparation that will remove all trace of the scent, so that hopefully, your cat will not be drawn back to the area again.

In the case of an older cat, it may simply be that she has difficulty getting into her litter box easily. A design that provides more straightforward access is to be recommended, because this may help to overcome the problem. If it persists, it may be worthwhile to have your

cat checked by your vet to ensure that there is not a more serious underlying medical problem.

If you have recently moved to a new home, your cat may soil around the house to mask out traces of a previous cat that may have lived there. It is a good idea to have any furnishings, especially carpeting, cleaned beforehand to eliminate all traces of the former feline occupant's scent. Curtains that reach down to ground level should also be cleaned for this reason.

Be sure to place the litter box for your cat in a quiet and yet easily accessible part of your new home. It is important to direct your cat's attention to this area, especially if she was previously allowed to roam freely outdoors and is not used to using a litter box. Otherwise, she may soil around the home. Most cats will use a litter box almost instinctively, but there are also sprays that you can use to attract your cat to this area.

Avoid placing the litter box close to your cat's food and water, because it may then be ignored. Although there are special scoops that allow you to clean the litter, bear in mind that a cat will bypass a dirty litter box, and choose a site elsewhere in the home, so it may be better simply to discard the soiled cat litter and box lining. *See also: Spraying.*

Spraying

Cats of both sexes may spray, but this behavior is more commonly associated with tom cats. They are especially inclined to use their urine as a territorial marker, and this helps explain why they need to be neutered if they are be kept in the home. Their urine is particularly pungent and a tom will spray regularly to reinforce his territorial claims, both in and out of the home. Urine is very important for cats for communication purposes. The urine of unneutered queens contains pheromones, which are chemical attractants. These draw male cats from a wide area, who home in on the scent to find a would-be mate. Otherwise the naturally solitary nature of cats would cause difficulties in locating a mate.

A Cat's Tale
Keep To The Path!

Cats will often spray prominent landmarks such as tree stumps or fence posts adjacent to the traditional paths that neighboring cats use to cross the backyard. This serves as a warning to all strangers that the territory is occupied.

When cleaning up after a cat that has urinated indoors, it is very important to use a product that not only cleans, but also removes all trace of the scent—just like rain washes away a cat's scent outdoors. Otherwise your cat is likely to return to the spot and spray again to reinforce its scent. Special products for this purpose are available from pet stores, but the real solution is to have your pet neutered. Females will sometimes spray too, although they are less inclined to do so, compared with males.

Standing Up

Some cats get into the habit of standing up against you—using your legs for support—when they want to greet you, rather than just rubbing against your legs. This reflects how cats normally greet each other by rubbing their noses together. It is actually a manifestation of a behavior seen in kittens. They reach up to acknowledge their mother when she comes back, and she will put her head down toward her offspring. If you sit down immediately after coming in, your cat is most likely to leap up onto the arm of the chair alongside you to be closer to your face.

Some cats also learn to beg, in a similar way to dogs, in search of a tidbit. They can soon become conditioned to behave this way if you respond. It is not necessarily a good idea though, because not only will you be pestered for food at every meal by your cat, but this could easily result in her becoming overweight quickly.

Stealing Food

It is common for cats to leap up onto work surfaces, such as counters or tables, if they can smell tasty food. Even wrapping meat or fish in packaging will not prevent your cat from being able to smell its presence. But generally they prefer fresh-cooked food, which may give off a stronger odor. Some cats even manage to paw open the door of the refrigerator and help themselves to food after watching you.

The risk of stealing will be greater if you use canned food, and store the uneaten portion of the can in the refrigerator, because it tends to focus your cat's attention on the refrigerator as a source of food. If this happens, the best solution to keep your food safe is to invest in a refrigerator lock. There is no risk that your cat will become aggressive if she does manage to steal raw meat, although feeding a cat raw meat is definitely not recommended, because of the risk of acquiring harmful bacteria such as salmonella.

As a general safety rule, always try to exclude your cat from the kitchen when cooking. Don't be inclined to give your pet a tidbit at this stage because you will soon be accompanied by an eager companion hoping for something to eat whenever you are cooking. This may actually be dangerous, especially when you are carrying hot food from the oven to the work surface. You could end up scalding both your pet and yourself badly under these circumstances if you drop the food.

A cat may also be at risk of burning herself if she leaps up onto the stove, which is another reason why it so important to keep her away from the kitchen while cooking. Also avoid leaving food out where it could attract your cat. There is nothing worse than preparing a special meal for guests, only to find that your cat has helped herself to the main course, such as a cooked salmon, before you sit down to eat at the table. Be aware of where your cat is in the home when you are setting the table, and as an additional precaution, keep chairs tucked in under the table. Otherwise, it will be very easy for your cat to jump up and check what is on the table.

Sucking Wool

This can easily develop into a serious behavior problem; its origins trace back to kittenhood. Wool is more likely to be a problem than other materials because it is soft and strands can be

pulled back easily. It also contains a natural oil, called lanolin. A young cat will start pawing with each front foot in turn at the wool. It then starts to suck on several strands, ultimately focusing on a strand that has begun to work loose.

This behavior mimics the way a kitten will gently paw at a teat to encourage milk flow; the strand of wool has a texture similar to a nipple. Not only does this become a habitual problem, but a cat can start to swallow strands of wool, which can create an obstruction in the digestive tract, just like a fur ball.

Wool-sucking is especially common in orphaned kittens, presumably because they were denied close contact with their mother. But it is nowhere near as common in those that were fostered, rather than reared by hand. It is also most likely to be encountered in kittens that were weaned at a relatively early age. There is also a breed predisposition, with the problem being especially prevalent in Siamese. Although cats often lose interest in wool-sucking as they mature, it can become a lifelong worry in some cases.

As a result, it is important to avoid using wool of any kind as bedding for young kittens and to discourage your pet from sucking at your woolen clothing while sitting on your lap. Also, do not leave woolen clothes around in places such as a

chair, where they could easily attract your cat's attention. It is virtually impossible to cure wool sucking if you allow this to develop into a habit, so it is vital to prevent the problem.

Teeth Chattering
Cats often behave this way when they are feeling frustrated, particularly when they are sitting on a windowsill and can see a bird on a bush outside, but cannot reach it because of the glass. It is not a sign that your pet is cold.

Tracking Prey
Cats hunt by relying primarily on their acute senses of sight and sound to locate prey, as well as scent. It is not unusual for a cat to move its head slightly from side to side, after it has stalked undetected within reach of its prey. This marks a final assessment before the cat launches into a strike. Its binocular vision (see page 89) allows the cat to jump with great precision. Moving her head slightly beforehand gives the clearest picture of where the prey is located.

Accidents

With the increase in traffic on the roads, more cats are involved in accidents, so there is a higher risk that you will be confronted with this situation. Even if your pet is not involved, it is still a distressing experience.

The first step is to remove the cat from further danger and try to confine her securely. Even though she may know you well, she will be in severe shock and may act abnormally. Try to reassure her by speaking quietly in a calm way, and move slowly so as not to alarm her.

Dealing With Shock

Adrenaline will be surging through the victim's body because of the shock and pain, so she may be aggressive and will not take kindly to being handled. If she is up and able to move it is a good sign, although it offers no guarantee that there are no internal injuries. One of

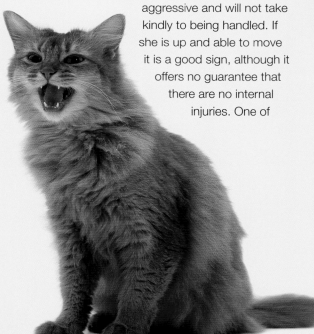

the biggest risks is internal hemorrhaging—perhaps as a result of a ruptured spleen, which causes blood to seep into the abdominal cavity. The color of the cat's gums can provide an indicator of internal bleeding, although shock means that the gums are likely to be pale rather than their typical pinkish shade. There is little point trying to assess the injuries yourself, because this will only distress her further and there will be little that you can do. You may notice areas of damaged skin, but it is possible to overcome very severe injuries with skin grafts. You need to get your pet to the vet urgently for further treatment.

Handling Your Cat

Find a pair of thick gardening gloves, so you can transfer the cat to her cat carrier without being badly scratched or bitten. Whether or not your cat is conscious after an accident, try to keep her body horizontal when you lift her. A torn diaphragm is a very common injury in cats that have been involved in road traffic accidents. The diaphragm acts as a partition between the chest and abdomen, but if it is torn, the body organs can slip through with potentially serious consequences.

Your vet will conduct a series of tests to assess the state of your cat's injuries, and give treatment as necessary. This may mean that your pet will be incapacitated for some time and you may have to nurse her for several weeks. Try to stick to a familiar routine as much as possible. Cats sometimes lose confidence after an accident, and spending time with your pet at this stage can be crucial in aiding her to recover quickly.

Helping Her Recovery

If your cat's neck is sore, she may be more willing to feed from your outstretched hand, rather than bending down to the food bowl. Raising the food bowl and the water container off the floor slightly may also help. Your cat cannot be left to wander unsupervised outdoors if she has been badly injured so you will need to buy a litter box. Even if you already have one, you may need a more straightforward design, because an injured cat may have difficulty in clambering into a covered litter box.

Regular grooming sessions are important, especially if she cannot groom herself effectively. Watch your pet carefully to discover her limitations—it may not necessarily just be a matter of keeping her coat in good condition, you may also need to clean her ears. Do not poke these with anything, just use a damp (not wet) cotton ball to wipe around the exposed inner surface of the ear. You may want to clean around the mouth as well, especially if the fur is soiled with wet food. If your cat is immobilized for any

length of time, keep an eye on her claws. If they are not worn down, they will start to curl over at the tip, which will make walking difficult and painful—especially if the claws dig into her toes.

There can be long-term consequences after a road accident—a fractured hip may make it difficult for a queen to give birth without a caesarean section, for instance. Check with your vet to see if he or she anticipates any such difficulties. Cats generally display remarkable powers of recovery, but do not assume that your pet will learn from an unpleasant experience. In areas where traffic is busy and a cat is allowed outdoors, she may be involved in more than one accident during her lifetime—which can easily be curtailed as a consequence.

Index

Acknowledgments

Photo Credits

147 © Piers Cavendish / ardea.com
8, 55, 95, 156, 160, 165 © John Daniels / ardea.com
114 © Jean Paul Ferrero / ardea.com
148 © Francois Gohier / ardea.com
116 © Rolf Kopflle / ardea.com
13, 37, 102 (bottom), 107 (right), 126, 145, 159, 186 (right) © Jean-Michel Labat / ardea.com
154 right: © George Reszeter / ardea.com
161 right: © Duncan Usher / ardea.com

9 (bottom), 11 (top) © Mary Evans Picture Library

97 (top left, top middle, top right), 98, 99, 100, 103, 104 (left and right), 105, 120 (top), 121 (top and bottom), 122 (bottom), 128 (top), 134, 136 (left and right), 137, 143 (bottom) © Marc Henrie

10, 25, 75, 82, 150 (top) ph Chris Everard © Ryland Peters & Small
48 (top), 64 (bottom), 144, 161 (left), 162, 163 ph Chris Tubbs © Ryland Peters & Small
6, 11 (bottom), 40 (top), 58, 89, 153, 181 ph Andrew Wood © Ryland Peters & Small

1, 2, 4, 5, 9 (top), 12, 15, 16, 17, 18, 19, 20, 21, 22, 23, 24 (top and bottom), 26, 27, 28, 29, 30, 31 (left and right), 32 (top and bottom), 33, 34, 35, 38, 39, 40 (bottom), 41, 42, 43 (left and right), 44 (top and bottom), 45, 46 (top left, top middle, top right and bottom), 47, 48 (bottom), 50 (top and bottom), 51 , 53, 56, 57, 59, 60, 61, 62, 63, 64 (top), 65, 66, 67, 68 (top and bottom), 69 (top and bottom), 70, 71 (top and bottom), 72, 73, 74, 76, 77, 78, 79, 81, 82 (top), 83, 84 (top and bottom), 95, 86, 87, 88, 90 (top and bottom), 92, 93, 96, 101, 102 (top), 106, 109 (top and bottom), 110, 112, 113 (bottom), 115 (top and bottom), 119 (top and bottom), 120 (bottom), 122 (top), 123, 125 (top, bottom left, bottom right), 127, 128, 129, 130, 131 (top and bottom), 133, 135, 138, 139, 140, 141, 149, 150 (bottom), 151, 154 (left), 155, 157 (left and right), 158, 163, 166, 167 (left, middle, right), 170 (left and right), 171 (left and right), 172, 173 (left and right), 174, 176, 178 (left and right), 179 (left and right), 182 (left and right), 183, 184 (left and right), 185 (left and right), 186 (left), 187 © Jane Burton / Warren Photographic

107 (left), 108, 113 (top), 117, 124, 132, 143 (top) © Tetsu Yamazuki